Teacher Edition

Reveal
MATH®
Language Development
Handbook
Course 2

McGraw Hill

mheducation.com/prek-12

Send all inquiries to:
McGraw-Hill Education
STEM Learning Solutions Center
8787 Orion Place
Columbus, OH 43240

ISBN: 978-0-07-697590-7 (Language Development Handbook, Course 2, Teacher Edition)
MHID: 0-07-697590-8 (Language Development Handbook, Course 2, Teacher Edition)
ISBN: 978-0-07-902925-6 (Language Development Handbook, Course 2, Student Edition)
MHID: 0-07-902925-6 (Language Development Handbook, Course 2, Student Edition)

Visual Kinesthetic Vocabulary® is a registered trademark of
Dinah-Might Adventures, LP.

6 7 8 9 10 LKV 27 26 25 24 23 22 21

Contents

How to Use This Book

Module 1 Proportional Relationships

Module 2 Percents

Module 3 Operations with Integers

Module 4 Operations with Rational Numbers

Module 5 Simplify Algebraic Expressions

Module 6 Write and Solve Equations

Module 7 Write and Solve Inequalities

Module 8 Geometric Figures

Module 9 Measure Figures

Module 10 Probability

Module 11 Sampling and Statistics

McGraw-Hill Education's Guiding Principles for Supporting English Learners

McGraw-Hill Education is committed to providing English Learners appropriate support as they simultaneously learn content and language. As an organization, we recognize that the United States is a culturally and linguistically diverse country. Moreover, this diversity continues to increase, with corresponding growth in the number of English Learners (ELLs). In 2012–2013, an estimated 4.85 million ELLs were enrolled US schools; this subgroup now makes up nearly 10% of the total public school enrollment (Ruiz-Soto, Hooker, and Batalova, 2015). In fact, ELLs are the fastest growing student population in the country, growing 60% in the last decade, compared with only 7% growth of the general student population (Grantmakers for Education, 2013). Perhaps most interesting of all, the vast majority of ELLs – 85% of prekindergarten through fifth grade ELLs, and 62% of high school ELLs – were born in the United States (Zong & Batalova, 2015). These US-born ELLs may be first-, second-, or third-generation students with strong ties to their cultural roots.

A great many ELLs come to school with a variety of rich linguistic and cultural backgrounds from Spanish-speaking communities and countries all throughout the Americas. In addition to Spanish, there are some ELLs that come to school speaking fluent or limited Spanish in addition to an indigenous language native to North, Central and South America. In addition, schools experience native speakers from numerous other backgrounds and languages—the most common other languages being Cantonese, Hmong, Korean, Vietnamese, and Haitian Creole. While over 70% of ELLs come to school speaking Spanish as their native language, as a group, ELLs speak nearly 150 languages (Baird, 2015). The experiences and identities acquired in the context of ELLs' homes and communities can transform the simplest classroom into a unique cultural and linguistic microcosm.

English Learners' success in learning a second language is influenced by a variety of factors besides the instructional method itself, including individual, family, and classroom characteristics; school and community contexts; the attributes of the assessment used to measure progress; and whether the language acquired is a national or foreign language (August & Shanahan, 2006; Genesee, Lindholm-Leary, Saundes, & Christian, 2006). For instance, children's initial levels of proficiency in their home language(s), along with English, influence new language acquisition (August, Shanahan, Escamilla, K., 2009) as does the quality of school support (Niehaus & Adelson, 2014) and the characteristics of the language learners' first and second languages (Dressler & Kamil, 2006)

Given these factors, there is a pressing need for fundamental principles that guide the support of ELLs as they acquire content and develop language. Drawing upon extensive research in the field, McGraw-Hill Education has developed nine guiding principles for supporting English Learners at all grade levels and in all disciplines.

Guiding Principles

- ✓ Provide Specialized Instruction

- ✓ Cultivate Meaning

- ✓ Teach Structure and Form

- ✓ Develop Language in Context

- ✓ Scaffold to Support Access

- ✓ Foster Interaction

- ✓ Create Affirming Cultural Spaces

- ✓ Engage Home to Enrich Instruction

- ✓ Promote Multilingualism

Proficiency Level Descriptors

	Interpretive (Input)		Productive (Output)	
	Listening	**Reading**	**Writing**	**Speaking**
An Entering/Emerging Level ELL • New to this country; may have memorized some everyday phrases like, "Where is the bathroom", "My name is....", may also be in the "silent stage" where they listen to the language but are not comfortable speaking aloud • Struggles to understand simple conversations • Can follow simple classroom directions when overtly demonstrated by the instructor	• Listens actively yet struggles to understand simple conversations • Possibly understands "chunks" of language; may not be able to produce language verbally	• Reads familiar patterned text • Can transfer Spanish decoding somewhat easily to make basic reading in English seem somewhat fluent; comprehension is weak	• Writes labels and word lists, copies patterned sentences or sentence frames, one- or two-word responses	• Responds non-verbally by pointing, nodding, gesturing, drawing • May respond with yes/no, short phrases, or simple memorized sentences • Struggles with non-transferable pronunciations.
A Developing/Expanding Level ELL • Is dependent on prior knowledge, visual cues, topic familiarity, and pretaught math-related vocabulary • Solves word problems with significant support • May procedurally solve problems with a limited understanding of the math concept.	• Has ability to understand and distinguish simple details and concepts of familiar/ previously learned topics	• Recognizes obvious cognates • Pronounces most English words correctly, reading slowly and in short phrases • Still relies on visual cues and peer or teacher assistance	• Produces writing that consists of short, simple sentences loosely connected with limited use of cohesive devices • Uses undetailed descriptions with difficulty expressing abstract concepts	• Uses simple sentence structure and simple tenses • Prefers to speak in present tense.
A Bridging Level ELL • May struggle with conditional structure of word problems • Participates in social conversations needing very little contextual support • Can mentor other ELLs in collaborative activities.	• Usually understands longer, more elaborated directions, conversations, and discussions on familiar and some unfamiliar topics • May struggle with pronoun usage	• Reads with fluency, and is able to apply basic and higher-order comprehension skills when reading grade-appropriate text	• Is able to engage in writing assignments in content area instruction with scaffolded support • Has a grasp of basic verbs, tenses, grammar features, and sentence patterns	• Participates in most academic discussions on familiar topics, with some pauses to restate, repeat, or search for words and phrases to clarify meaning.

Collaborative Conversations

Students engage in whole-class, small-group, and partner discussions during every lesson. The chart below provides prompt frames and response frames that will help students at different language proficiency levels interact with each other in meaningful ways.

You may wish to post these frames in the classroom for student reference.

Core Skills	Prompt Frames	Response Frames
Elaborate and Ask Questions	Can you tell me more about it? Can you give me some details? Can you be more specific? What do you mean by…? How or why is it important?	I think it means that… In other words… It's important because… It's similar to when…
Support Ideas with Evidence	Can you give any examples from the text? What are some examples from other texts? What evidence do you see for that? How can you justify that idea? Can you show me where the text says that?	The text says that… An example from another text is… According to… Some evidence that supports that is…
Build On or Challenge Partner's Ideas	What do you think of the idea that…? Can we add to this idea? Do you agree? What are other ideas/points of view? What else do we need to think about? How does that connect to the idea…?	I would add that… I want to follow up on your idea… Another way to look at it is… What you said made me think of…
Paraphrase	What do we know so far? To recap, I think that… I'm not sure that was clear. How can we relate what I said to the topic/question?	So, you are saying that… Let me see if I understand you… Do you mean that…? In other words… It sounds like you are saying that…
Determine the Main Idea and Key Details	What have we discussed so far? How can we summarize what we have talked about? What can we agree upon? What are main points or ideas we can share? What relevant details support the main points or ideas? What key ideas can we take away?	We can say that… The main idea seems to be… As a result of this conversation, we think that we should… The evidence suggests that…

Strategies for Classroom Discussion

Providing multiple opportunities to speak in the classroom and welcoming all levels of participation will motivate English learners to take part in class discussions and build oral proficiency. These basic teaching strategies will encourage whole class and small group discussions for all language proficiency levels of English learners.

 ## Wait time/Different Response

- Be sure to give students enough time to answer the question. They may need more time to process their ideas.
- Let them know that they can respond in different ways depending on their levels of proficiency. Students can:
  - Answer in their native language; then you can rephrase in English
  - Ask a more proficient ELL speaker to repeat the answer in English
  - Answer with nonverbal cues.

 ## Elaborate

- If students give a one-word answer or a nonverbal clue, elaborate on the answer to model fluent speaking and grammatical patterns.
- Provide more examples or repeat the answer using proper academic language.

 ## Elicit

- Prompt students to give a more comprehensive response by asking additional questions or guiding them to get an answer, such as can you tell me more?
- This strategy is very effective when students are asked to justify or explain their reasoning.

 ## Asking about Meaning

- Repeating an answer offers an opportunity to clarify the meaning of a response.
- Repeating an answer allows you to model the proper form for a response. You can model how to answer in full sentences and use academic language.
- When you repeat the answer, correct any grammar or pronunciation errors.

ENTERING/EMERGING

- What is _____?
- What does _____ mean?
- _____ is _____.
- _____ means _____.

DEVELOPING/EXPANDING

- Could you tell me what _____ means?
- _____ is similar to _____.
- _____ is another way of saying _____.

BRIDGING

- Could you give me a definition of _____?
- Can you point to the evidence from the text?
- What is the best answer? Why?

Talk about Level of Understanding

ENTERING/EMERGING	• I understand./I got it.
	• I don't understand this word/sentence.
DEVELOPING/EXPANDING	• Could you tell me what _____ means?
	• _____ is another way of saying _____.
BRIDGING	• I think I understand most of it.
	• I'm not sure I understand this completely.

 Justify Your Reasoning

ENTERING/EMERGING	• I think _____.
DEVELOPING/EXPANDING	• My reasons are _____.
BRIDGING	• I think _____ because _____.

 Agreeing with Someone's Reasoning

ENTERING/EMERGING	• I agree with your reasons or point.
DEVELOPING/EXPANDING	• I agree that _____.
BRIDGING	• I have the same reasons as _____. I think that _____.

 Disagreeing with Someone's Reasoning

ENTERING/EMERGING	• I don't agree with your reasons.
DEVELOPING/EXPANDING	• I don't agree that _____.
BRIDGING	• I can see your point. However, I think that _____.

How to Use the Teacher Edition

The suggested strategies, activities, and tips provide additional language and concept support to accelerate English learners' acquisition of academic English.

English Learner Instructional Strategy

Each English Learner Instructional Strategy can be utilized before or during regular class instruction.

Categories of the scaffolded support are:

- Vocabulary Support
- Language Structure Support
- Sensory Support
- Graphic Support
- Collaborative Support

The goal of the scaffolding strategies is to make each individual lesson more comprehensible for ELLs by providing visual, contextual and linguistic support to foster students' understanding of basic communication in an academic context.

Lesson 1 Unit Rates Involving Complex Fractions

English Learner Instructional Strategy

Vocabulary Support: Frontload Academic Vocabulary

Before the lesson, write and discuss these multiple-meaning words: *complex* and *reciprocal*. Define each word, using realia, demonstrations, and illustrations to support understanding.

Complex fractions are simplified when the numerator and denominator are both integers. Write the word *integer*. Explain that an integer can be either positive or negative. Draw a number line numbered from −5 to 5. Then read aloud each number as you point to it. Explain that each number is an integer because it does not include a fraction or decimal amount. Then point to the negative signs that precede −5 through −1. Explain how the signs show that these numbers are negative, or less than zero, and how numbers without a negative sign

---

Since ELLs benefit from visual references to new vocabulary, many of the English Learner Instruction Strategies suggest putting vocabulary words on a Word Wall. Choose a location in your classroom for your Word Wall, and organize the words by module, by topic, or alphabetically.

English Language Development Leveled Activities

These activities are tiered for Entering/Emerging, Developing/Expanding, and Bridging leveled ELLs. Activity suggestions are specific to the content of the lesson. Some activities include instruction to support students with lesson specific vocabulary they will need to understand the math content in English, while other activities teach the concept or skill using scaffolded approaches specific to ELLs. The activities are intended for small group instruction, and can be directed by the instructor, an aide, or a peer mentor.

English Language Development Leveled Activities

Entering/Emerging	Developing/Expanding	Bridging
Word Knowledge	**Anchor Chart**	**Partners Work/Pairs Check**
Write: $2 \cdot 2 \cdot 5 = 20$ and *factored form*. Underline *factor*. Point to 2 and ask, *Is 2 a factor?* **yes** Repeat with 5. Point to 20 and ask, *Is 20 a factor?* **no** Help students define *factor*. Then circle the *ed* in *factored*. Explain that sometimes the *-ed* ending ~~Teacher talk is~~ noun into an adj ~~italicized.~~ is a describing word. Show and explain how *factored* describes *form*: The *factored form* of an expression is the *form* that shows its *factors*. Finally, write expressions in both their factored and unfactored forms. Ask, *Which is the factored form?* Students point to the answer.	Draw a four-column chart on the board, with these column heads: Factor (noun), Factor (verb), Factored Form, Greatest Common Factor. Then, under each head, have students help you write the following: 1) a math definition for the term, using students' words; 2) a sentence that uses the term in ~~Student talk is~~ context. For example, ~~boldfaced.~~ the following are responses for the noun *factor*: **1) Definition: a number or variable multiplied by another number or variable to form a product; 2) One factor of 21 is 7; 3) Factors of 21 are 1, 3, 7, 21.**	Have partners work together to write word problems involving monomials. Tell them their word problems must include information that can be represented in a linear expression and a solution that involves factoring the expression. Then have students trade their problems with another pair and solve the word problem they receive. Finally, have partners check answers with the pair who wrote the problem.

Multicultural Teacher Tip

You may see some ELLs using a method other than the factor trees commonly used in U.S. classrooms to find factors. In Mexico, students are taught to draw a vertical line. On the left side, they write the number to be factored, and then the first prime factor is written on the

18	2

Multicultural Teacher Tip

These tips provide insight on academic and cultural differences you may encounter in your classroom. While math is the universal language, some ELLs may have been shown different methods to find the answer based on their native country, while cultural customs may influence learning styles and behavior in the classroom.

How to Use the Student Edition

Each student page provides ELL support for vocabulary, note taking, and writing skills. These pages can be used before, during, or after classroom instruction. A corresponding page with answers is found in the teacher resources.

Word Cards

Students define each vocabulary word or phrase and write a sentence using the term in context. Space is provided for Spanish speakers to write the definition in Spanish.

A blank word card template is provided for use with non-Spanish speaking ELLs.

Lesson 4 Vocabulary
Discounts

Use the word cards to define each vocabulary word or phrase and give an example.

Word Cards	
discount	**descuento**
Definition	Definición
Example Sentence	

Vocabulary Squares

Vocabulary squares reinforce the lesson vocabulary by having students write a definition, write a sentence using the vocabulary in context, and create an example of the vocabulary. Suggest that students use translation tools and write notes in English or in their native language on the cards as well for clarification of terms. Encourage students to identify and make note of cognates to help accelerate the acquisition of math concepts in English.

Lesson 1 Vocabulary
Rational Numbers

Use the vocabulary squares to write a definition, a sentence, and an example for each vocabulary word.

	Definition
repeating decimal	
Example	Sentence

	Definition
bar notation	
Example	Sentence

Three-Column Chart

Three-column charts concentrate on English/ Spanish cognates. Students are given the word in English. Encourage students to use a glossary to find the word in Spanish and the definition in English. As an extension, have students identify and highlight other cognates which may be in the definitions.

A blank three-column chart template is provided for use with non-Spanish speaking ELLs.

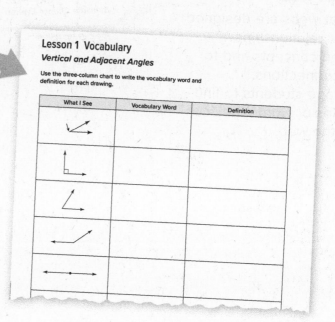

Lesson 1 Vocabulary
Vertical and Adjacent Angles

Use the three-column chart to write the vocabulary word and definition for each drawing.

What I See	Vocabulary Word	Definition

Definition Map

The definition maps are designed to address a single vocabulary word, phrase, or concept. Students should define the word in the description box. Most definition maps will ask students to list characteristics and examples. Others, as shown at the left, will ask students to perform other tasks. Make sure you review with students the tasks required.

Lesson 2 Vocabulary
Area of Circles

Use the definition map to list qualities about the vocabulary word or phrase.

Vocabulary

semicircle

Description

Characteristics

Draw examples of semicircles.

How to Use the Student Edition *continued*

Concept Web

Concept webs are designed to show relationships between concepts and to make connections. Encourage students to find examples or words they can use in the web.

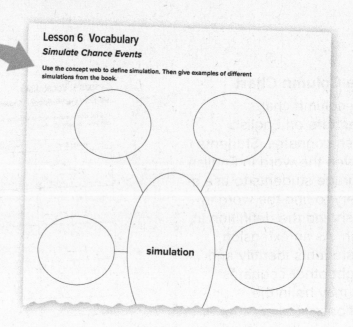

Lesson 6 Vocabulary
Simulate Chance Events

Use the concept web to define simulation. Then give examples of different simulations from the book.

simulation

Cornell Notes

Cornell notes provide students with a method to take notes thereby helping them with language structure. Scaffolded sentence frames are provided for students to fill-in important math vocabulary by identifying the correct word or phrase according to context.

Lesson 3 Notetaking
Subtract Linear Expressions

Use Cornell notes to better understand the lesson's concepts. Complete each sentence by filling in the blanks with the correct word or phrase.

Questions	Notes
1. How do I subtract linear expressions?	I subtract _____ terms. I use _____ pairs if needed.
2. What is the additive inverse of a linear expression?	The additive inverse of a linear expression is an expression with terms that are _____. The sum of a linear expression and its additive inverse is _____.

English/Spanish Cognates used in Course 2

English	Spanish	VKV Page Number
absolute value	valor absoluto	VKV7
acute triangle	triángulo acutángulo	
additive inverse	inverso aditivo	VKV7
algebra	álgebra	
algebraic expression	expresión algebraica	
Associative Property	propiedad asociativa	
bar notation	notación de barra	VKV11
base	base	
center	centro	VKV25
circle	círculo	VKV25
circumference	circunferencia	VKV25
coefficient	coeficiente	VKV15
common denominator	común denominador	VKV11
Commutative Property	propiedad conmutativa	
complementary angles	ángulos complementarios	
complementary events	eventos complementarios	
composite figure	figura compuesto	VKV27
compound event/simple event	evento compuesto/evento simple	
cone	cono	VKV21
congruent	congruente	VKV21
constant	constante	
constant of proportionality	constante de proporcionalidad	
cylinder	cilindro	
define a variable	definir una variable	
dimensional analysis	análisis dimensional	
Distributive Property	propiedad distributiva	
equation	ecuación	
equilateral triangle	triángulo equilátero	
equivalent equation	ecuación equivalente	VKV19
experimental probability/theoretical probability	probabilidad experimental/probabilidad teórica	VKV35
factor	factorizar	VKV15
factored form	forma factorizada	VKV15
graph	graficar	VKV9
isosceles triangle	triángulo isosceles	
lateral surface area	área de superficie lateral	VKV29
linear expression	expresión lineal	VKV17

English	Spanish	VKV Page Number
monomial	monomio	VKV17
Multiplicative Identity Property	propiedad de identidad de la multiplicación	
negative	negativo	
nonproportional/proportional	no proporcional/proporcional	
obtuse angle	ángulo obtuso	
obtuse triangle	triángulo obtuso	
opposites	opuestos	VKV9
ordered pair	par ordenado	
origin	origen	
percent error	porcentaje de error	VKV5
plane	plano	VKV21
population	población	VKV37
prism	prisma	
probability	probabilidad	
property	propiedad	
proportion	proporción	VKV3
pyramid	pirámide	
radius/diameter	radio/diámetro	VKV27
rational number	número racional	VKV13
regular pyramid	pirámide regular	VKV31
relative frequency	frecuencia relative	
scale	escala	
scale factor	factor de escala	VKV24
scale model	modelo a escala	VKV23
scalene triangle	triángulo escaleno	
semicircle	semicirculo	VKV27
simple interest	interés simple	
simplify	simplificar	
simulation	simulación	VKV33
solution	solución	VKV19
statistics	estadística	VKV37
supplementary angles	ángulos suplementarios	
surface area	área de superficie	
term	término	
triangle	triángulo	
uniform probability model	modelo de probabilidad uniforme	
vertex	vértice	
x-coordinate/y-coordinate	coordenada x/coordenada y	

Lesson _____

Use the word cards to define each vocabulary word or phrase and give an example.

Word Cards

_____	_____

Definition

_____

_____

_____

Example Sentence

_____

_____

Word Cards

_____	_____

Definition

_____

_____

_____

Example Sentence

_____

_____

Lesson _____

Use the three-column chart to organize the vocabulary in this lesson.

English	Native Language	Definition

Lesson 1 · Unit Rates Involving Ratios of Fractions

English Learner Instructional Strategy

Vocabulary Support: Frontload Academic Vocabulary

Before the lesson, write and discuss these multiple-meaning words: *complex* and *reciprocal*. Define each word, using realia, demonstrations, and illustrations to support understanding.

Complex fractions are simplified when the numerator and denominator are both integers. Write the word *integer*. Explain that an integer can be either positive or negative. Draw a number line numbered from −5 to 5. Then read aloud each number as you point to it. Explain that each number is an integer because it does not include a fraction or decimal amount. Then point to the negative signs that precede −5 through −1. Explain how the signs show that these numbers are negative, or less than zero, and how numbers without a negative sign are positive, or greater than zero or zero.

Math Language Routine: Compare and Connect

Think aloud about Example 1, using comparative terms such as *all, some,* or *none* to model how the four methods compare. Encourage input from students regarding how estimates can be useful, even if they are not the actual solution.

English Language Development Leveled Activities

Entering/Emerging	Developing/Expanding	Bridging
Developing Oral Language List the following items: $\frac{8}{2}$; $8 \div 2$; 8 divided by 2. Then point to each and say, *All of these mean the same thing.* In the first item, point to 8 and say *eight,* point to the fraction bar and say *divided by,* then point to 2 and say *two.* Repeat the process with the other two items. Then ask, *What is eight divided by two?* Have students respond using this sentence frame: _____ **divided by** _____ **equals** _____. Now write: $\frac{9}{3}$; $9 \div 3$; 9 divided by 3. Have students say each expression and then say its solution using the sentence frame.	**Building Oral Language** Write the following: $\frac{\frac{1}{4}}{2}$ and $\frac{1}{4} \div 2$. Point to both items and say, *These mean the same thing.* In Item 1, point first to $\frac{1}{4}$ and say *one-fourth,* then to the larger fraction bar and say *divided by,* finally point to 2 and say *two.* Next, in Item 2, point first to $\frac{1}{4}$ and say *one-fourth,* then to the division sign and say *divided by,* finally point to 2 and say *two.* Now say, *Let's simplify the expresion.* Work through the steps to simplify the complex fraction. Have students respond, using this sentence frame: _____ **divided by** _____ **is the same as** _____ **times** _____. **The answer is** _____.	**Think-Pair-Share** Have partners work together to write a word problem whose solution involves dividing one fraction by another fraction. If students have difficulty writing a problem, refer them back to Examples 3-5 in the book. Then ask students to exchange problems with another pair. Have partners work together to solve the problem they received. Then ask them to present the word problem and solution to the class. Allow peers to ask questions and have the presenter justify their solution.

NAME _____ DATE _____ PERIOD _____

Lesson 1 Vocabulary
Unit Rates Involving Ratios of Fractions

Use the definition map to list qualities about the vocabulary word or phrase.
Sample answers are given.

Vocabulary

> complex fraction

Characteristics

> can have both
> the numerator and
> the denominator as
> fractions

Description

> a fraction where the
> numerator and/or
> denominator are fractions

> simplified when
> the numerator
> and denominator are
> integers

$$\frac{\frac{1}{2}}{\frac{1}{5}} = \frac{5}{2} \text{ or } 2\frac{1}{2}$$

$$\frac{9}{\frac{3}{4}} = 12$$

Write and simplify examples of complex fractions.

Lesson 2 Understand Proportional Relationships

English Learner Instructional Strategy

Language Structure Support: Tiered Responses

As you work through the lesson, be sure to check ELL students' understanding during every step. You can do this by asking questions that elicit responses appropriate to their level of English acquisition. Instructions for Entering/Emerging students must be short and clear, using known vocabulary, so they can respond by pointing or saying **yes/no**. Developing/Expanding students can give short answers and may attempt simple sentences. Bridging students can create longer sentences and synthesize more information in English.

Emerging/Emerging students: *Point to the square that shows 1 part. Does this show a proportional relationship?*
Developing/Expanding students: *How many parts of _____? How many equal sections? How many ____ does each section represent?*
Bridging students: *What is the ratio of ____ to ____? How do you know this is proportional?*

Math Language Routine: Critique, Correct, and Clarify

Make a false claim for students to critique; for example, *If* two *pair of socks cost $5.98 and three pair cost $6.98, this is a proportional relationship*. Ask students to correct the statement, explaining how they know it is incorrect. Revisit this routine throughout the lesson.

English Language Development Leveled Activities

Entering/Emerging	Developing/Expanding	Bridging
Listen and Identify	**Act It Out**	**Anchor Chart**
Invite four students to come forward. Hand each student one pencil. Then hand each student three sheets of paper. On the board, draw a table showing the ratio of 1 pencil to 3 sheets of paper. Say, *This is a proportional relationship*. Have students chorally repeat **proportional relationship**. Then hand each student between one and four paper clips. Draw a table showing that the number of paper clips per student is a nonproportional relationship. Say, *This is a nonproportional relationship. It is **not** proportional.*	On the board, draw a table showing the ratio 1:5. Divide students into small groups of three or four students and distribute manipulatives to each group. Have them use manipulatives to show a proportional relationship, with 1 part equal to 6. Then ask, *How many are in 5 parts?* **30** Then have students use the manipulatives to show a nonproportional relationship, or a ratio that is not equivalent to 1:5. Have students use the following sentence frames: **The ratio ____ to ____ is not equivalent to one to five. So it is nonproportional.**	Have students work in small groups to create anchor charts for proportional and nonproportional relationships. Their charts should include definitions and examples. Have students display their charts. Then ask one volunteer from each group to explain why their group's examples show proportional and nonproportional relationships.

NAME _____ DATE _____ PERIOD _____

Lesson 2 Notetaking
Understand Proportional Relationships

Use Cornell notes to better understand the lesson's concepts. Complete each sentence by filling in the blanks with the correct word or phrase.

Questions	Notes
What is a proportional relationship?	Two quantities are in a __proportional relationship__ when the two quantities __vary__ and have a constant __ratio__ between them. Example: A recipe calls for 1 tablespoon of baking soda to 4 cups of flour. Elise uses 4 tablespoons of baking soda for 16 cups of flour. Is this a proportional relationship? ⊢1 tbsp⊣ baking soda [1] flour [1][1][1][1] ⊢------- 4 cups -------⊣
Words I need help with: **See students' words.**	⊢4 tbsp⊣ baking soda [4] flour [4][4][4][4] ⊢------- 16 cups -------⊣ The ratio __was__ maintained, so this __is__ a proportional relationship.

Summary

What are other ways to show proportional relationships bedsides bar diagrams?

See students' examples.

_____

_____

_____

Lesson 3 Tables of Proportional Relationships
English Learner Instructional Strategy

Vocabulary Support: Activate Prior Knowledge

Before the lesson, write *proportional* and *nonproportional* and their Spanish cognates, *proporcional* and *no proporcional,* respectively, on the Word Wall. Introduce the words, and provide math examples to support understanding. Utilize other appropriate translation tools for non-Spanish speaking ELLs. Then circle *non-* in *nonproportional.* Explain that *non-* is a prefix that means "not." Point out that when *non-* is added to *proportional,* it forms a word that is an antonym of *proportional.* Then tell students that *proportional* is a multiple-meaning word. Discuss how this word is used within the context of design, as well as math.

Math Language Routine: Stronger and Clearer Each Time

Have students individually write their responses to the Talk About It question on Student Book page 25, then pair up with another student to refine and clarify their responses through conversation. Students then revise their initial written responses and repeat with a new partner.

English Language Development Leveled Activities

Use the following problem with these leveled activities: *Andrew earns $18 per hour for mowing lawns. Is the amount of money he earns proportional to the number of hours he spends mowing?*

Entering/Emerging	Developing/Expanding	Bridging
Look, Listen, and Identify	**Academic Word Knowledge**	**Show What You Know**
Write the ratios for the problem on the board and say, *This is a ratio. Each ratio compares the amount of money earned to the hours Andrew works.* Point to each ratio and say, for example, *The **ratio** is eighteen to one.* Have students repeat each ratio chorally, using this sentence frame: **The ratio is _____.** Ask, *Are all of these ratios **equivalent**, or equal?* **yes** Then circle all the ratios and say, *All of these ratios are **equivalent**. So, the relationship between the amount of money Andrew earns to the hours he works is **proportional**.* Have students repeat chorally.	Repeat the Emerging Level activity. Say The relationship between the cost of boxes of cards and the number of boxes purchased are shown by following ratios. Write $\frac{\$15}{1}$, $\frac{\$25}{2}$, $\frac{\$35}{3}$, and $\frac{\$45}{4}$ on the board. Ask, *Are all the ratios **equivalent?** **no** Say, *The ratios are **not** equivalent, so the relationship between the cost and the number of boxes of cards is **nonproportional**.* Have students repeat chorally.	Divide students into pairs, and give each pair an index card. Ask students to describe a relationship that is proportional and write three ratios that represent the relationship. Then have them repeat the process for a nonproportional relationship. Ask partners to present both sets to the class, explaining why each is proportional or nonproportional.

NAME _____ DATE _____ PERIOD _____

Lesson 3 Vocabulary

Tables of Proportional Relationships

Use the three-column chart to organize the vocabulary in this lesson. Write the
word in Spanish. Then write the definition of each word. Sample answers are given.

English	Spanish	Definition
proportional	proporcional	the relationship between two ratios with a constant rate or ratio
nonproportional	no proporcional	the relationship between two ratios with a rate or ratio that is not constant
constant of proportionality	constante de proporcionalidad	a constant ratio or unit rate of two variable quantities

Lesson 4 Graphs of Proportional Relationships
English Learner Instructional Strategy

Vocabulary Support: Anchor Chart

Before the lesson, add the terms *coordinate plane, ordered pair, x-coordinate, y-coordinate,* and *origin* and their Spanish cognates, *plano de coordenadas, par ordenado, coordenada* x, *coordenada* y, and *origen,* respectively, to a Word Wall. Introduce the words, and provide math examples to support understanding.

Have students preview the illustration of a four-quadrant coordinate plane on the student page. On an anchor chart, write the following associated vocabulary: *grid, intersect, quadrants, zero points, x-axis, y-axis, negative numbers, positive numbers, graph.* Use the illustration and realia, as needed, to explain each term. Then have students help you write a definition for the term to be added to the anchor chart.

Math Language Routine: Collect and Display

As students discuss the questions *How are graphs of proportional and nonproportional linear relationships alike? How are they different?,* write key words and phrases you hear, such as *graph, proportional relationship, table, origin, nonproportional relationship, linear,* and *straight.* Display the words and phrases for student reference throughout the lesson. Update the collection with other relevant terms and new understandings as the lesson progresses.

English Language Development Leveled Activities

Entering/Emerging	Developing/Expanding	Bridging
Word Knowledge Draw a coordinate plane. Then write: (1, 2). Point to the numbers and say, *This is an **ordered pair.*** Have students repeat chorally. Explain that an ordered pair always appears inside parentheses. Point to the parentheses. Have students repeat chorally. Then explain how the order in which the numbers appear is important. Say, *The **first** number coordinates with the **x-axis**.* Point to the *x*-axis. Then say, *The **second** number coordinates with the **y-axis**.* Point to the *y*-axis. Show students how to use the ordered pair to plot a point on the coordinate plane.	**Show What You Know** Write the chart below on the board. <table><tr><td>Number of Books</td><td>Number of Students</td></tr><tr><td>0</td><td>0</td></tr><tr><td>2</td><td>1</td></tr><tr><td>4</td><td>2</td></tr><tr><td>6</td><td>3</td></tr></table> Draw the first quadrant of a coordinate plane. Label the *x*-axis "Books" and the *y*-axis "Students." Invite volunteers to write ordered pairs based on the numbers in the chart and then plot them on the coordinate plane. Ask, *Is the number of books proportional to the number of students?* Have students respond: **The number of books [is/is not] proportional to the number of students.**	**Number Game** Draw two first quadrant coordinate planes. Label the axes with increments of 5. Divide students into two teams. Have both teams face away from the board as you write these ordered pairs: (0, 0), (1, 7), (2, 14), (3, 21). Then tell students they will do a relay race: First, one student from each team plots the point described in the first ordered pair. Then that student passes the marker to a team member, to plot the point described by the next ordered pair. Students continue this way until all points are plotted. The final student correctly identifies the points' relationship by writing *proportional* or *nonproportional.* **proportional** The first team to finish wins!

NAME _____ DATE _____ PERIOD _____

Lesson 4 Vocabulary

Graphs of Proportional Relationships

Use the word bank to identify the parts of the coordinate plane. Then draw an arrow from the word to the part of the coordinate plane it describes.

Word Bank			
origin	ordered pair	Quadrant III	Quadrant I
x-axis	x-coordinate	y-axis	y-coordinate

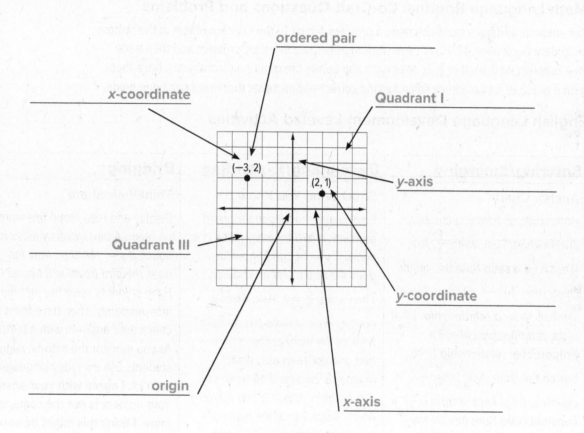

Lesson 5 Equations of Proportional Relationships

English Learner Instructional Strategy

Vocabulary Support: Cognates

Before the lesson, add the phrase *constant of proportionality* and the Spanish cognate, *constant de proporcionalidad*, to a Word Wall. Introduce the phrase and provide math examples to support understanding. Ask students to refer to a dictionary or glossary to recall the meaning of *constant*. Then write: *proportion/proportionality.* Explain that the first word in the pair carries the main meaning for the second word in the pair. Then help students relate the meanings of the paired words.

Math Language Routine: Co-Craft Questions and Problems

Pair students and have them co-create a problem similar to the Check problem at the bottom of Student Book page 44. Have them work together to solve their problem and then trade their problem with another pair. After each pair solves the other pair's problems, have them form a group of four to check solutions and correct any mistakes that may have been made.

English Language Development Leveled Activities

Entering/Emerging	Developing/Expanding	Bridging
Anchor Chart Have students help you create an anchor chart. First, write: $\frac{y}{x}$. Ask, *What is $\frac{y}{x}$?* **a ratio** Note this on the chart. Then write: $\frac{y}{x} = k$. Say, *These symbols show a* **relationship**. *What is the* **relationship** *called?* **a proportional relationship** Note this on the chart. Ask, *When $\frac{y}{x}$ equals k, what* **kind** *of ratio is $\frac{y}{x}$?* **a constant ratio** Note this on the chart. Finally, ask, *In a proportional relationship, what do we call the* **constant ratio**? **constant of variation, constant of proportionality** Note this on the chart.	**Show What You Know** Display and read aloud this word problem: *A bird travels y miles in x hours. If y = 14x, then how far does the bird travel in 3 hours?* Then write: $\frac{y}{x} = k$. Ask, *What is another way to write this formula? Look at the word problem for a hint.* **y = kx** Then ask, *What number is constant?* **14** Next, say, *The problem says the bird travels 3 hours. Does 3 take the place of y or x in the formula?* **x** *So, what does y equal?* **42** Now write: $\frac{42 \text{ miles}}{3 \text{ hours}}$. Say, *If it takes 3 hours to travel 42 miles, what is the constant ratio?* $\frac{14}{1}$	**Think-Pair-Share** Display and read aloud this word problem: *A bird travels y miles in x hours. If y = 14x, then how far does the bird travel in 3 hours?* Have students solve the problem independently. Then have them check their answers with a partner. As you monitor the activity, suggest students use everyday language, such as, **I agree with your answer. Your answer is not the same as mine. I think this might be wrong. Did you remember to _____ ? Why don't you try _____?** Once partners agree on an answer, invite a volunteer to share the problem's solution.

Multicultural Teacher Tip

Encourage ELLs to share traditions, stories, songs, or other aspects of their native culture with the other students in class. You might even create a "culture wall" where all students can display cultural items. This will help create a classroom atmosphere of respect.

NAME _____ DATE _____ PERIOD _____

Lesson 5 Vocabulary
Equations of Proportional Relationships

Use the word cards to define each vocabulary word, and complete the Example
sentence. Sample answers are given.

Word Card

constant of proportionality	constant de proporcionalidad

Definition

a constant ratio or unit rate of

two variable quantities

Definición

una razón constante o tasa

por unidad de dos cantidades

variables

Example

In the equation $y = kx$, the variable ___*k*___ represents the

constant of proportionality.

Word Card

unit rate	tasa unitaria

Definition

a rate that is simplified so

that it has a denominator of

1 unit

Definición

tasa simplificada para que

tenga un denominador

igual a 1

Example

In a proportional relationship, the ___constant of proportionality___

is the same as the unit rate.

Lesson 6 Solve Problems Involving Proportional Relationships

English Learner Instructional Strategy

Vocabulary Support: Utilize Resources

Before the lesson, review the Word Wall for vocabulary introduced earlier in the lesson. In particular, point out the base word proportion that appears in some of the words and phrases they learned, such as proportional relationship and constant of proportionality. Then add proportion and its Spanish cognate, proporción, to the Word Wall. Introduce its meaning and provide examples to support understanding.

Then preview the lesson with a "chapter walk." Guide students as they skim the pages for math and nonmath vocabulary that may be unfamiliar or difficult to understand. Look at the pages with them and assess their understanding by asking, *Do you know what _____ means?* Create a list of words that need to be introduced or reviewed. Then have students take turns using multilingual glossaries to preteach the vocabulary to all students.

Math Language Routine: Discussion Supports

As students engage in discussing the Talk About It questions on page 50, restate statements they make as a question to seek clarification and to confirm comprehension, providing validation or correction when necessary.

English Language Development Leveled Activities

Use the following problem with these leveled activities: For every four cats examined at the vet's office, there are five dogs examined. If the vet's office examines 92 cats in a week, how many dogs were examined the same week?

Entering/Emerging	Developing/Expanding	Bridging
Modeled Talk	**Report Back**	**Public Speaking**
Work as a group to solve the problem. As each step is completed, tell what you did, emphasizing correct pronunciation. Then have students repeat the key word. For example, say, *The **ratio** of cats to dogs is 4 to 5.* Then have students chorally repeat: **ratio**. Say, *I will write an **equation** to solve.* Have students chorally repeat: **equation**. Continue in this way, modeling pronunciation for each step in the solving process.	Ask pairs to work through the problem together. Number pairs 1 to 3, and assign a different number to each solving method (table, equation, or graph). Have pairs solve using their assigned method. Then have them report back to the class about how they solved their problem, using these sentence frames: **The unit rate is _____. We divided _____ by _____. We multiplied _____ by _____. We graphed the points _____ and _____. The constant of probability is _____. _____ dogs were examined.**	Have students work independently to solve the problem using any of the three methods: table, equation, or graph. Afterward, survey students to determine which methods they used. Organize students into small groups to discuss which method they used and why. Then ask volunteers to stand and express their opinions about which method was best for solving the problem. Remind them to speak clearly, politely, and look at the audience. Offer feedback about pronunciation, grammar, and the use of formal language.

NAME _____ DATE _____ PERIOD _____

Lesson 6 Notetaking
Solve Problems Involving Proportional Relationships

Use the concept web to show three different ways to solve the proportional relationship problem.

Use a table.

Number of vans	1	3	9
Number of students	8	24	72

____Nine____ vans are needed.

Use an equation.

$y = kx$

$24 = k(3)$

$k = 8$

$72 = 8x$

$x = 72 \div 8$

$x = 9$

____Nine____ vans are needed.

A group of 24 students will ride in 3 vans to get to the zoo. If 72 students are going to the zoo, how many vans are needed? Assume the relationship is proportional.

Use a graph

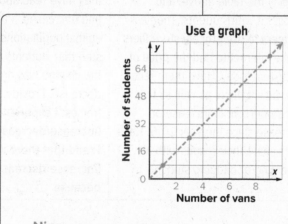

____Nine____ vans are needed.

Lesson 1 Percent of Change
English Learner Instructional Strategy

Sensory Support: Mnemonics

Remind students that a percent of change can be an *increase* or *decrease*. Write *increase* and *decrease* on the board, then underline the *in* in *increase*. Tell students the *in-* prefix can mean "into." Model *into* by dropping pennies into a jar. Say, *I put pennies **into** the jar. I **add** pennies to the jar. This is an **increase**.* Write a plus sign next to *increase*. Then underline the *de* in *decrease* and tell students the *de-* prefix can mean "away." Model *away* by taking pennies out of the jar. Say, *I take pennies **away** from the jar. I **subtract** from the pennies in the jar. This is a **decrease**.* Write a minus sign next to *decrease*.

Math Language Routine: Three Reads

Ensure comprehension of the Check problem on page 68 of the Student Book.
1st Read: Make sure students understand the difference between when a spring is resting and when it is compressed.
2nd Read: Support students in understanding that they are being asked the percent of difference in length between when the spring is resting and when it's compressed.
3rd Read: Brainstorm ways to find the percent of decrease, rounded to the nearest percent.

English Language Development Leveled Activities

Entering/Emerging	Developing/Expanding	Bridging
Word Knowledge Write and say: *compare*. Have students repeat. Coach them on forming the *r*-controlled vowel sound in the second syllable, which starts as /ā/ and glides into /r/. Then, make a T-chart with the headings Same and Different. Hold up two objects. Say, *Let's **compare**. Let's tell how they are the **same** and how they are **different**.* Discuss similarities. Say, *These are the **same**. Both [are/have] _____.* List similarities under Same. Then discuss differences. Say, *These are **different**. One [is/has] _____.* List differences under Different.	**Share What You Know** <table><tr><td>Item</td><td>Cost in 2015</td></tr><tr><td>Gallon of milk</td><td>$3.31</td></tr><tr><td>Loaf of bread</td><td>$1.44</td></tr><tr><td>Gallon of gas</td><td>$2.40</td></tr></table> Display the table above, and discuss it with students. Then ask partners to use grocery store fliers or the Internet to find the price of each item today. Have them record the current price, as well as the price's percent of increase or decrease since the year 2015. Have pairs share their results with an emerging or bridging student.	**Building Oral Language** Have partners discuss what they know about percents of change. Have them share times in which they have experienced price increases or decreases, or times they have read about increases and decreases in things like sales, animal populations, and so on. Be sure that students identify whether the change was an increase or a decrease. Provide these sentence frames: **I experienced a percent of [increase/decrease] when _____. I read that there was a percent of [increase/decrease] in _____ because _____.**

Multicultural Teacher Tip

You may experience ELLs who appear to listen closely to your instructions and exhibit verbal and/or nonverbal confirmation that they understand the concepts. It may become clear during the lesson that they did not actually understand. This may be due to a student coming from a culture in which the teacher is regarded as a strong authority figure.

NAME _____ DATE _____ PERIOD _____

Lesson 1 Vocabulary
Percent of Change

Use the vocabulary squares to write a definition, a sentence, and an example for each vocabulary word.

percent of change	Definition
	a ratio that compares the change in a quantity to the original amount
Example	**Sentence**
$\frac{2}{40} = 5\%$	A $40 sweater decreased in price by $2. The percent of change is 5%.

percent of increase	Definition
	a positive percent of change
Example	**Sentence**
$\frac{5}{10} = 50\%$	A $10 shirt had a price increase of $5. The percent of increase is 50%.

percent of decrease	Definition
	a negative percent of change
Example	**Sentence**
$\frac{15}{75} = 20\%$	A $75 jacket is on sale for $60. The percent of decrease is 20%.

Course 2 · Module 2 *Solve Percent Problems* **7**

Lesson 2 Tax
English Learner Instructional Strategy

Graphic Support: Word Webs

Write *Tax* in the middle of a word web. Discuss what students know about this word. Write down students' responses. Tell students that tax money is paid to the government, and the government uses the money to provide services to taxpayers. Tax is usually a percent of an amount of money, such as a price of a good.

Students will learn two types of tax in this lesson: income and sales tax. Add *sales tax* to an outer circle on the web. Ask students what they pay sales tax for. Write down their ideas. Be aware that some states do not charge sales tax and not all states charge sales tax for the same items. Add *income tax* to another circle on the outside of the web. Discuss what *income* is, and point out that the word is a compound word: *in/come*. Be aware that some states do not impose an income tax on residents. The vocabulary phrase *payroll tax* can be a sub-circle of *income tax*. It is the tax a company pays for all its employees.

Math Language Routine: Information Gap

Have pairs of students play *Find My Cost*. Student *A* writes the price of an item on a card; Student *B* writes a tax rate on a different card. Students exchange cards and individually determine the final cost of the item including the tax. Encourage students to challenge each other's answers and to refine or clarify their findings through conversation.

English Language Development Leveled Activities

Entering/Emerging	Developing/Expanding	Bridging
Developing Oral Language	**Building Oral Language**	**Make Cultural Connections**
Display the word web created in the ELL instructional strategy above. Say simple sentences about goods, services, and wages, such as *I am paid $10 per hour. What tax will I pay?* or *I will buy a new computer. What tax will I pay?* Have students tell whether you will pay a sales tax or an income tax. Review the frame: **You will pay [a sales/an income] tax.**	Repeat the Entering/Emerging activity. Once students are clear on the differentiation between sales and income tax, have them use a sentence frame to practice conditional sentences. For example, **If you (are paid $10 per hour), you will (pay an income tax).**	Have students ask their families about the taxes that are collected in their home countries. What type of taxes are collected? What goods and services are taxed? How much is sales tax? How much is income tax? Have students report their findings to the group.

NAME _____ DATE _____ PERIOD _____

Lesson 2 Vocabulary

Tax

Use the definition map to write a list qualities about the vocabulary word or phrase. Sample answers are given.

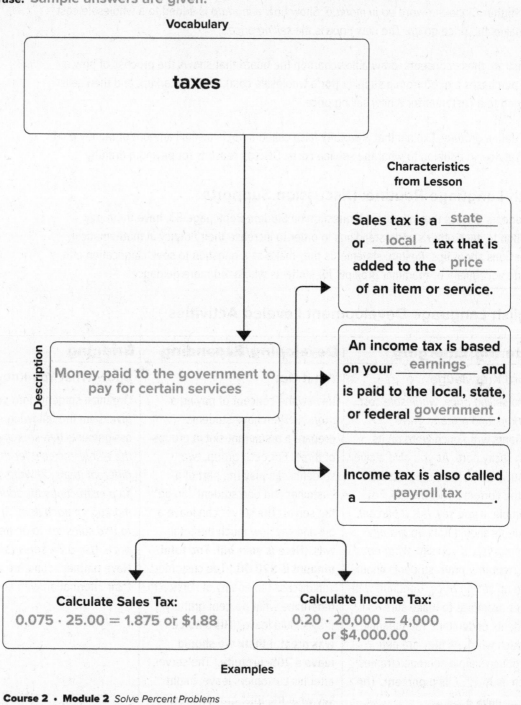

Vocabulary

taxes

Characteristics from Lesson

Sales tax is a __state__ or __local__ tax that is added to the __price__ of an item or service.

Description

Money paid to the government to pay for certain services

An income tax is based on your __earnings__ and is paid to the local, state, or federal __government__.

Income tax is also called a __payroll tax__.

Calculate Sales Tax:
0.075 · 25.00 = 1.875 or $1.88

Calculate Income Tax:
0.20 · 20,000 = 4,000 or $4,000.00

Examples

Lesson 3 Tips and Markups

English Learner Instructional Strategy

Vocabulary Support: Frontload Academic Vocabulary

Review *selling price*. Preteach *wholesale cost, markup,* and *gratuity*. Write and say each term. Define *wholesale cost*. Explain that when the store buys an item from a supplier, they pay a *wholesale cost*. Ask, *Do you think the selling price is higher or lower than the wholesale cost?* **higher** Circle the word *up* in *markup*. Show how a *markup* is added to a wholesale cost and makes the price go *up*. The new price is the *selling price*.

To illustrate these concepts, draw a flowchart on the board that shows the process of how a store purchases a good from a supplier (for a wholesale cost), adds a markup, and then sells the good to a customer for a new selling price.

Then define *gratuity*. Explain that a *gratuity* (also called a *tip*) is a small amount of money paid for a service, in addition to what the service costs. Discuss reasons for paying a gratuity.

Math Language Routine: Discussion Supports

As students discuss the Talk About It question on Student Book page 83, have them pay attention to each other's understandings in order to increase their fluency in mathematical discussions about tips. Restate statements they make as a question to seek clarification and provide vocabulary or grammar prompts for students who need more guidance.

English Language Development Leveled Activities

Entering/Emerging	Developing/Expanding	Bridging
Word Knowledge	**Act It Out**	**Show What You Know**
Write *selling price, wholesale cost, markup,* and *gratuity*. Have students write each word on its own sticky note. As you give a clue about a word, have students hold up the correct sticky note(s). For example, if you say, *It is a percent,* students should hold up *gratuity* and *markup*. If you say, *What does the customer pay?,* students should hold up *selling price*. Continue with other examples to make sure students understand the meaning of each word. As they are able, introduce simple sentence frames, such as **A _____ is a percent. The _____ pays a _____.**	Review the concept of paying a *gratuity*. Then have students prepare a restaurant skit in groups of three. For each group, two students can play the part of a customer and one student can be the server. The server can leave a bill and say how much the total was. (**Here is your bill. The total amount is $20.00.**) The customers can discuss the quality of service to determine what percent gratuity they should leave. (**His service was great. I think we should leave a 20% gratuity.**) The server, after his customers leave, might say what the total gratuity was. (**Wow, they left me $4.00!**)	Organize students into pairs, and give them the following assignment: *1) Research and record the wholesale cost for three different items. 2) Write step-by-step instructions for adding a 20% markup on each item. 3) Show how to add sales tax to an item's selling price. Use a 7% sales tax rate.* Have partners compare and check their information with another pair.

NAME _____ DATE _____ PERIOD _____

Lesson 3 Vocabulary
Tips and Markups

Use the three-column chart to organize the vocabulary in this lesson. Write the
word in Spanish. Then write the correct terms to complete each definition.

English	Spanish	Definition
gratuity	gratificacíon	An additional amount of money paid in return for a <u>service</u> . It is also called a <u>tip</u> .
markup	margen de utilidad	The amount the <u>price</u> of an item is <u>increased</u> above the price the store paid for the item. selling price — <u>wholesale cost</u> = markup
selling price	precio de venta	The amount the customer <u>pays</u> for an item.
wholesale cost	el costo de venta por mayor	The amount a <u>store</u> pays for an item.

Lesson 4 Discounts

English Learner Instructional Strategy

Vocabulary Support: Word Knowledge

Before the lesson, write *discount* on the board. Underline *count* and demonstrate its meaning. For example, say, *I will count my fingers.* Point to each finger as you count it, from one to ten. Then say, *I will count my students.* Gesture toward each student as you count him or her. Next, circle the letters *dis* in *discount.* Tell students that *dis-* is a prefix that means "opposite." Then explain that, within the context of this lesson, *discount* is a noun that means "an amount deducted from, or not counted in, the selling price." It is also a verb that means "to deduct from, or not count in, the selling price." It also has an adjective form, *discounted* (as in *discounted price*), that is used to describe items whose prices have been reduced, or lowered.

Math Language Routine: Collect and Display

As students discuss the Examples, write key words and phrases you hear, such as *discount, original price, percent of discount, sale price,* and *clearance price.* Display the words and phrases for student reference throughout the lesson. Update the collection with new understandings as the lesson progresses.

English Language Development Leveled Activities

Entering/Emerging	Developing/Expanding	Bridging
Signal Words and Phrases Help students differentiate the phrases *for sale* and *on sale.* Write both phrases on the board, and have students say them with you. Then explain that items *for sale* are items to sell. Show students photos of different vendors selling goods. Point to a vendor and say, for example, *This person has food for sale. This person has art for sale.* Then explain that items *on sale* are sold at a discounted price. Show store ads with the word *Sale* on them. Point to items in the ads and say, for example, *This toaster is on sale. Its discount price is ____. This cereal is on sale. Its discount price is ____.*	**Word Knowledge** Some students may confuse the terms *rate of discount, discount,* and *discount price.* Have students write each term on an index card. Then work as a class to define the terms using students' words. **Sample responses: *rate of discount*—a percent; *discount*—the amount of money the price is reduced; *discount price*—the cost after subtracting the discount.** Finally, encourage students to write notes and illustrations on their index cards, to help with remembering a term's definition. (Example: A synonym for *discount price* is *sale price,* because it is the price of an item *on sale.*)	**Word Lists** Write: *sale price, selling price, discount, regular price, discount price, 40% off, markdown, discounted price, 40% discount* on the board. Have partners use these terms to create a synonyms word web. Show how to start by drawing a large circle and labeling it "Synonyms." Then demonstrate adding to the web by connecting other circles to the center circle. Tell students that each circle should contain two synonyms. Have partners compare their finished web with that of another pair of students. **sale price/discount price; selling price/regular price; discount/markdown; 40% off/40% discount**

NAME _____ DATE _____ PERIOD _____

Lesson 4 Vocabulary
Discounts

Use the word cards to define each vocabulary word or phrase and give an example.

Word Cards

discount

Definition
the amount by which the
regular price of an item is
reduced

Example Sentence
A $40 sweater was marked down during the store's sale. The
discount was $5.

descuento

Definición
cantidad que se le rebaja al
precio regular de un artículo

Word Cards

markdown

Definition
an amount by which the
regular price of an item is
reduced

Example Sentence
A $40 sweater was marked down during the store's sale. The
markdown was $5.

rebaja

Definición
una cantidad por la cual el
precio regular de un artículo
se reduce

Lesson 5 Interest

English Learner Instructional Strategy

Language Structure Support: Multiple-Meaning Words

Before the lesson, write *simple interest* and its Spanish cognate, *interés simple* on the Word Wall. Introduce the words, and provide math examples. Point out that both words within the term have multiple meanings. Use real-world objects, photos, and demonstrations to support understanding. Then write: *principal* on the board. Tell students that this is a multiple-meaning word, as well as a homophone for *principle*. Discuss how *principal* is more commonly used to refer to a person who is the head of a school. Show students the mnemonic, *A princi**pal** is a **pal** (friend)* to remind them that *principal* sometimes refers to a person. Then discuss its math meaning. Finally, explain that *principle* generally means "a rule or truth."

Math Language Routine: Stronger and Clearer Each Time

Have students individually write their response to the question *How is the interest earned related to the length of time and the interest rate*?, then pair up with another student to refine and clarify their response through conversation. Students then revise their initial written response and repeat with a new partner.

English Language Development Leveled Activities

Entering/Emerging	Developing/Expanding	Bridging
Word Knowledge	**Partners Work/Pairs Share**	**Share What You Know**
Demonstrate the meaning of *borrow*. Approach a student and say, *I **need** a math book.* Show that you don't have a math book. Then use gestures to communicate that you would like to use the student's book, while asking, *May I please **borrow** your math book?* When the student lets you have his or her book, say, *Thank you for letting me **borrow** your book.* Use the same procedure to request use of other classroom items, such as a pencil or paper. Then write: *take out a loan, buy on credit.* Use illustrations and role-playing to explain and show that these phrases name ways to borrow money.	Write and then read aloud this word problem: *Bryan borrows $6,000. His interest rate is 6.5% for 6 years. Dana borrows $5,000. Her interest rate is 8% for 6 years. Who will pay more interest? How much money will this person pay? Who will have to pay back more money in all? How much money will this person pay?* Have partners work together to solve the problem. Provide these sentence frames for forming responses: _____ **will pay more interest. [He/She] will pay $ _____. _____ will pay more money in all. [He/She] will pay a total of $_____.** Then have partners compare answers with another pair.	Write and then read aloud this word problem: *Connor invests $2,500 at 3.5% for 4 years. Gabriela invests $4,000 at 2.5% for 3 years. Who will earn more interest on the money invested? How much money will he or she earn? Who will have more money at the end of the 3 or 4 year term? How much money will he or she earn?* Ask partners to work together to write step-by-step instructions for solving the problem. Then have them compare solutions with another pair of students. Once they are sure their answers are correct, have them explain their solutions to an emerging or expanding student.

NAME _____ DATE _____ PERIOD _____

Lesson 5 Vocabulary
Interest

Use the concept web to identify and describe the parts of the simple interest formula. Sample answers are given.

Word Bank			
simple interest	principal	annual interest rate	time

(simple interest, the amount paid or earned for the use of money)

(principal, the amount of money deposited or borrowed)

$$I = prt$$

(annual interest rate, usually expressed as a percentage)

(time, expressed in years)

Lesson 6 Commissions and Fees

English Learner Instructional Strategy

Vocabulary Support: Build Background Knowledge

Write the following on the board: *goods, services, price, fee, commission*. Helps students understand that a good is a thing, such as food, furniture, etc. and that a service is something done for a person. For example, a car is a good, and if someone washes your car for you, it is a service. Have students give other examples of goods and services.

Ask, *What is a price?* **the amount you pay for something** Tell students that goods have a price. Have students give examples of items that have a price. (e.g., milk, cars, books) Then say, *The price for a service is called a fee.* Say the word *fee* and have students repeat. Ask, *What do we pay a fee for?* **possible responses: school fees (tuition), ATM fee, parking fee** Tell students that one type of fee is called a commission. It is an amount of money paid to a salesperson. It is the percent of the price of the item the salesperson sold. People who sell cars and houses receive a commission.

Math Language Routine: Co-Craft Questions and Problems

Pair students and have them co-create a problem similar to the Check problem at the bottom of Student Book page 110. Have them work together to solve their problem and then trade their problem with another pair. After each pair solves the other pair's problems, have them form a group of four to check solutions and correct any mistakes that may have been made.

English Language Development Leveled Activities

Entering/Emerging	Developing/Expanding	Bridging
Word Knowledge	**Developing Oral Language**	**Turn & Talk**
Have available several photos of goods and services (e.g., goods: toys, books, food, furniture; services: massage, doctor, dentist, lawn care service). Have students say **goods** or **services** for each photo you display.	Repeat the Entering/Emerging activity and have students use a sentence frame, such as, **A toy is a [good/service].** Then have students use another sentence frame to tell whether a price or a fee is paid for each one: **You pay a [price/fee] for a toy.**	Review the different ways that people can be paid for their work, such as *hourly wage, salary, commission only, salary plus commission*. After introducing each method, have students turn and talk to another student about the pros and cons to that method of payment. After all methods have been introduced and discussed, have partners tell each other which way they would prefer to be paid and why.

NAME _____ DATE _____ PERIOD _____

Lesson 6 Notetaking
Commission and Fees

Use Cornell notes to better understand the lesson's concepts. Complete each answer by filling in the blanks with the correct word or phrase.

Questions	Notes
1. What is a commission and how can I calculate it?	An employee sells _____ goods _____ or _____ services _____ for a company. The employee receives a commission. A _____ commission _____ is a payment equal to a _____ percent _____ of the amount of goods or services that an employee _____ sells _____. **Example** Carl sells a car for $25,000. His commission is 3%. His commission payment is $ _____ 750 _____.
2. What is a fee?	A fee is a _____ payment _____ for a service. A fee can be a _____ fixed amount _____, a _____ percentage _____ of the price, or _____ both _____. **Example** Marie bought a video game online for $50. The shipping fee was 10% of the cost of the game. The shipping fee was $ _____ 5.00 _____.

Summary
How can I use the percent equation to find commissions and fees? See students' work. _____ _____ _____

Lesson 7 Percent Error
English Learner Instructional Strategy

Language Structure Support: Tiered Questions

Write *percent* and its Spanish cognate, *por ciento,* on the board or a cognate chart. Review that *percent* means "for every 100" or "out of 100." Ask, *So, what is 20 percent?* If necessary, model and prompt students to say, **20 out of 100.** Repeat with several other examples.

Write *error.* Underline *err* and explain that the word means "to make a mistake." Write a few simple words or math equations on the board, including a few with spelling or calculation errors in them. For example, *persent, add, sudtract, multiply, devide,* $3 + 3 = 9, 3 \cdot 3 = 9.$ Ask questions according to students' level of English acquisition, such as:
Entering/Emerging: *Point to the error. Does this equation/word have an error?*
Developing/Expanding: *Which words have a spelling error?*
Bridging: *Find the errors and tell what the mistake is.*

Add *percent* and *error* to the Math Word Wall. Include visual examples.

Math Language Routine: Three Reads

Ensure comprehension of the Check problem on page 116 of the Student Book.
1st Read: Make sure students understand that they are being asked to determine the percent error of the estimated time for the family to reach their destination.
2nd Read: Support comprehension of the travel terms: *GPS system, destination,* and *stops.*
3rd Read: Brainstorm ways to find the percent error of the estimated time of travel.

English Language Development Leveled Activities

Entering/Emerging	Developing/Expanding	Bridging
Listen and Identify	**Round the Table**	**Share What You Know**
After introducing the concept, go over the steps for finding percent error one more time, perhaps writing the steps on the board. Review the steps by asking, *What do we find first?* **amount of error** *To find amount of error, do we add or subtract?* **subtract** Continue asking simple questions for which the answer is yes/no or a single word or phrase	Organize students in groups of four. Assign one student to be the "teacher." Give the group a percent error problem. Have the three "students" solve the problem with each student doing one step and the passing the paper to the next student to do the next step and so on. The "teacher" should be monitoring progress and offering assistance wherever needed.	Have partners create a "lesson plan" for teaching others how to find the percent error. First have them compile a list of information they must have (e.g., actual amount, estimate, amount of error) and prepare to introduce those concepts to others. Then have them prepare a numbered list of steps for finding the percent error. If time allows, have students partner with an Entering/Emerging or Developing/Expanding student and "teach" their lesson.

NAME _____ DATE _____ PERIOD _____

Lesson 7 Vocabulary
Percent Error

Use the vocabulary squares to write a definition, a sentence, and an example for each vocabulary word.

amount of error	Definition
	the positive difference between the estimate and the actual amount
Example	**Sentence**
43 years (actual age) — 38 years (estimate) = 5 years	Jesse guessed that Mr. Perez is 38 years old. Mr. Perez's actual age is 43. The amount of error is 5 years.

percent of error	Definition
	a ratio, written as a percent, that compares an amount of error (an estimate) to an actual amount
Example	**Sentence**
$\dfrac{\text{amount of error}}{\text{actual amount}} \cdot 100 = \dfrac{5}{38} \cdot 100$ $= 13.2\%$	The percent of error of Jesse's guess is 13.2%

Lesson 1 Add Integers

English Learner Instructional Strategy

Sensory Support: Physical Activities

On the board write *add* and *additive*. Point out the words' shared letters, and discuss how the words' meanings are related. Next, discuss *inverse*. Show students how inversing objects *turns* them into their opposites. For example, show students a hat. Say, *I will **turn** the hat to its **inverse** side.* Then turn the hat inside out and say, *Now the hat's **opposite** side shows.* Next, show students a coin that is heads side up. Say, *I will **turn** the coin to its **inverse** side.* Then turn the coin tails side up and say, *Now the coin's **opposite** side shows.* Then ask, *How do I form the additive inverse of a positive number?* Have students respond using this sentence frame: **Turn the positive number into a _____ number. (negative)**

After the lesson, add the terms *opposites* and *additive inverse* and their Spanish cognates, *opuestos* and *inverso aditivo*, respectively to a Word Wall with examples or drawings.

Math Language Routine: Stronger and Clearer Each Time

Have students individually write their response to the question *How can algebra tiles be used to model integer addition,* then pair up with another student to refine and clarify their response through conversation. Students then revise their initial written response and repeat with a new partner.

English Language Development Leveled Activities

Entering/Emerging	Developing/Expanding	Bridging
Act It Out Have students work in pairs. Give each pair a set of positive and negative counters. Then write these expressions on the board: $5 + (-3)$; $-6 + 2$; $-3 + 7$; $4 + (-6)$; $-4 + 4$. One student should model the expression with the counters. The other student uses the sentence frame, **The sum is [positive/negative] _____.** to state the value of the expression. For the next expression, students switch roles. Remind students to remove all zero pairs from their models.	**Number Game** Divide students into pairs, and distribute 6 to 7 index cards to each pair. Have pairs write *opposites* on one card and *additive inverses* on another. Then have them write a different integer on each of their remaining cards. A player takes a turn by drawing one word card and one integer card. Then he or she uses the cards to form a sentence. For example, if the word *opposite* and the integer -3 are drawn, the player might say, **Negative three and positive three are opposites.** Students take turns drawing cards and making sentences until all their integer cards have been used.	**Show What You Know** Have students work with a partner to think of different ways the concept of *opposites* has been used in their math lessons and in real-world situations in which they use math. For example, in their lessons they have worked with *positive integers* and *negative integers*, and at home they may have *added* and *subtracted* money from their savings accounts. Have partners create a list of antonym pairs, based on their discussion. **Sample responses: working forward/working backward, multiply/divide, deposit/ withdraw.** Then ask them to share their lists with the class.

NAME _____ DATE _____ PERIOD _____

Lesson 1 Vocabulary
Add Integers

Use the word cards to define each vocabulary word or phrase and give an
example. Sample answers are given.

Word Cards

opposites	opuestos
Definition	**Definición**
two integers that are the same	dos enteros que equidistant
distance from zero, but on	de cero, pero en direcciones
opposite sides of zero	opuestas

Example Sentence

The integers 2 and −2 are opposites; the sum of 2 and −2 is
zero.

Word Cards

additive inverse	inverso aditivo
Definition	**Definición**
two integers that are	dos enteros opuestos
opposites	

Example Sentence

The additive inverse of 2 is −2. The additive inverse of −2 is 2.

Lesson 2 Subtract Integers

English Learner Instructional Strategy

Vocabulary Support: Frontload Academic Vocabulary

Before the lesson, review the meaning of these terms, which students will encounter in word problems: *platform, diving board, diver, surface; temperatures, moon, maximum, minimum, degrees, Celsius, balance, account, bank, charged, fee; sea, surface, range, elevation*. Use photos, realia, and demonstrations to help support understanding. Discuss how many of the words have multiple meanings, and point out the antonyms (*maximum/minimum*) and the word with a homophone (*sea/see*). Ensure students are familiar with the symbol for *degrees* and the abbreviation for *Celsius*. Finally, show students Alabama, Louisiana, New Mexico, California, and Florida on a map of the United States.

Math Language Routine: Critique, Correct, and Clarify

Make a false claim for students to critique; for example, *A negative integer minus a negative integer is always a negative integer.* Ask students to correct the statement, explaining how they know it is incorrect. Revisit this routine throughout the lesson to provide reinforcement.

English Language Development Leveled Activities

Entering/Emerging	Developing/Expanding	Bridging
Build Background Knowledge Write the integers −3, 7, −8, −10, 9, 2 on the board. Point to the first and say, *This is negative three. What is the* **opposite** *of negative three?* **positive three** Invite a volunteer to come to the board and write: **3**. Continue in this manner until all the integers have been addressed. Next, write and say: 5 − (−1). Then say, *To subtract, I will add the* **opposite**. Write and say: 5 + 1 = 6. Continue by writing similar subtraction problems and having students tell you how to simplify them.	**Sentence Frames** Write 5 − (−1) on the board. Read the problem aloud. Then say, *To subtract negative one from positive five, I will add positive one to positive five.* Write: 5 + 1. Then say, *Positive five plus positive one equals positive six.* Continue by writing other subtraction problems on the board and having students tell how to simplify them. Have students use these sentence frames to form their explanations: **To subtract _____ from _____, add _____ to _____. The answer is _____.**	**Number Game** Divide students into pairs, and give each pair two number cubes. Each partner rolls both cubes and then writes a subtraction problem using the two numbers rolled. Each number rolled may be used in the problem as a positive integer or a negative integer. Repeat this process three times. Partners then exchange papers and simplify the problems by changing them into addition problems. Partners check each other's answers.

Multicultural Teacher Tip

ELLs may use an alternative algorithm when solving subtraction problems. For example, Latin American students may have been taught the equal additions method of subtraction. In the equal additions method, a problem such as 35 − 18 solved vertically would start with ten ones added to the top number (15 − 8) and then one ten is added to the bottom number (30 − 20), to get 7 and 10, or 17. Similarly, 432 − 158 would be solved as 12 − 8, 130 − 60, and 400 − 200 (4 + 70 + 200 = 274).

NAME _____ DATE _____ PERIOD _____

Lesson 2 Notetaking
Subtract Integers

Use the flow chart to review the process for subtracting integers.
Sample answers are given.

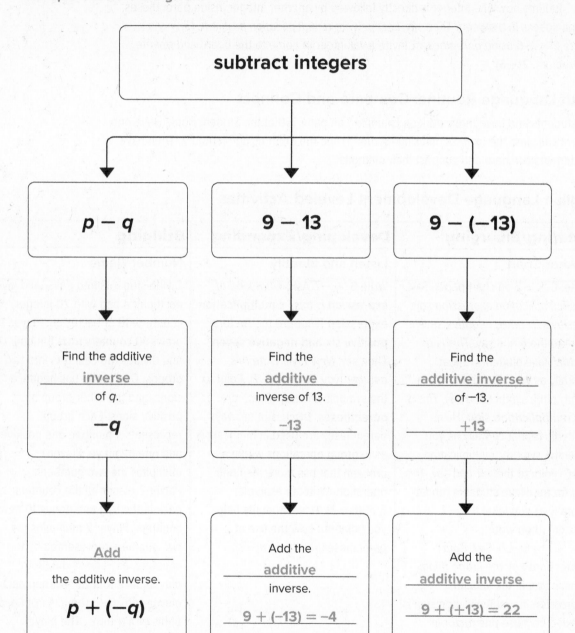

Lesson 3 Multiply Integers
English Learner Instructional Strategy

Vocabulary Support: Activate Prior Knowledge

Have students review the following statement and example: *The product of two numbers with different signs is negative.* 6(−4) = −24. Point out that *parentheses* are used in place of a multiplication symbol to indicate that two numbers should be multiplied by each other. Show students how one integer is directly followed by another integer inside parentheses, with no spaces in between. Then say, *Let's rewrite a multiplication problem. How can I rewrite 2 × −6 using parentheses?* Invite a volunteer to come to the board and rewrite the problem. **2(−6)**

Math Language Routine: Compare and Connect

Pair students and have them work on Example 1 on page 150 of the Student Book. Have one student calculate the expression using Method 1, and the other using Method 2. Then have the students compare and contrast their methods.

English Language Development Leveled Activities

Entering/Emerging	Developing/Expanding	Bridging
Anchor Chart Write: 6 × −7 on chart paper. Say, *This multiplication expression says "positive six times negative seven."* Point to the 6 and say, *This is a factor.* Have students repeat chorally as you label the 6 "factor." Point to the symbol and say, *This is the **multiplication sign**.* Have students repeat chorally as you label the symbol "multiplication sign." Point to the −7 and say, *This is a **factor**.* Have students repeat chorally as you label the −7 "factor." Then write: 6 × −7 = 6(−7). Say, *Both expressions say the **same** thing.* Explain that in the second expression, no multiplication sign is needed because one *factor* in *parentheses* follows the other *factor*, with no spaces in between. Label the parts of the second expression.	**Listen and Identify** Write 6 × −7. Ask, *What kind of **expression** is this?* **a multiplication expression** *What are the **factors**?* **positive six and negative seven** Then say, *Now I will write this another way.* Write: 6(−7). Point to the symbols and say, *These are **parentheses**.* Discuss other ways parentheses are used in math, such as to group operations within a problem that has more than one operation. Write an example: 6 × (1 − 8). Have students help you point out how the use of parentheses results in 6(−7).	**Number Game** Divide students into pairs, and give each pair a bag with 20 integer counters, 10 of each sign. Player 1 draws 10 counters from the bag and divides the counters into two groups. One group has negative signs, and the other group has positive signs. Each group represents a number, one positive and one negative. Player 1 multiplies the two numbers. Player 2 places all the counters back in the bag and draws 10 new counters. Player 2 multiplies the two numbers represented by the counters, as Player 1 did. Both players take four turns. Then each player adds the products from each of his or her turns. The player whose score is the *lowest* wins.

NAME _____ DATE _____ PERIOD _____

Lesson 3 Notetaking
Multiply Integers

Use Cornell notes to better understand the lesson's concepts. Complete each sentence by filling in the blanks with the correct word or phrase.

Questions	Notes
1. What sign is the product of two integers with different signs?	The product of two integers with _____different_____ signs is _____negative_____ .
2. What sign is the product of two integers with the same sign?	The product of two integers with the _____same_____ signs is _____positive_____ .

Summary

When is the product of two or more integers a positive number? See students' work.

_____

_____

_____

_____

_____

_____

_____

Lesson 4 Divide Integers

English Learner Instructional Strategy

Vocabulary Support: Activate Prior Knowledge

Before the lesson, remind students that addition and subtraction are related operations. Ask, *How are addition and subtraction related?* **They are opposites.** Then ask, *How is multiplication similar to addition?* **Multiplication is repeated addition.** Write: $(-4) + (-4) + (-4) = 3(-4)$. Discuss how adding -4 three times is like multiplying -4 by 3. Invite a volunteer to write the problem's solution: **−12.** Then say, *Like addition and subtraction, multiplication and division are opposites. If multiplication is repeated addition, what is division?* **repeated subtraction**

Finally, have students recall what they know about multiplying positive and negative integers. Ask, *When both factors have the same sign, is the product* **positive** *or* **negative**? **positive** *When is the product negative?* **when the factors have different signs** Tell students to keep this in mind as they learn about dividing integers.

Math Language Routine: Co-Craft Questions and Problems

Pair students and have them co-create a problem similar to the Apply problem on Student Book page 163. Have them work together to solve their problem and then trade their problem with another pair. After each pair solves the other pair's problems, have them form a group of four to check solutions and correct any mistakes that may have been made.

English Language Development Leveled Activities

Entering/Emerging	Developing/Expanding	Bridging
Listen and Identify Write: $-27 \div 3 = -9$. Say, *This is a **division** problem.* Then write and say: *dividend, divisor, quotient.* Point to -27 and say, *dividend.* Point to 3 and say, *divisor.* Point to -9 and say, *quotient.* Now write $-9 \times 3 = -27$. Say, *This is a multiplication problem.* Then point to the two problems you wrote and say, *These problems are **related**.* Point to -27 in the multiplication problem and say, *This is the product.* Then point to -27 in the division problem and ask, *What is -27 in the division problem?* **the dividend** Continue this process to help students relate 3 the *factor* to 3 the *divisor* and -9 the *factor* to -9 the *quotient*.	**Report Back** Divide students into pairs. Then write this problem on the board: $-12 \div 6 = -2$. Tell partners to write the problem on their own paper and then label each of its parts with one of these terms: *quotient, divisor, dividend.* Then ask them to write two multiplication problems that are related to the division problem. After students have had time to work, have them report their findings using these sentence frames: _____ **is the quotient.** _____ **is the divisor.** _____ **is the dividend.** Ask volunteers to write the two related multiplication problems on the board: **$-2 \times 6 = -12$, $6 \times (-2) = -12$**.	**Show What You Know** Write the following terms on the board: *factor, product, dividend, divisor, quotient.* Ask pairs of students to identify which terms apply to division and which apply to multiplication. Have partners write sentences telling how the multiplication terms relate to the division terms. For example: **The *product* of a multiplication problem becomes the *dividend* in a division problem.** Have students write a math example for each sentence, such as: **$-4 \times 3 = -12$; -12 is the product. $-12 \div 3 = -4$; -12 is the dividend.** Students can share their sentences and examples with the class.

NAME _____ DATE _____ PERIOD _____

Lesson 4 Notetaking
Divide Integers

Use the flow chart to review the process for dividing integers. Sample answers are given.

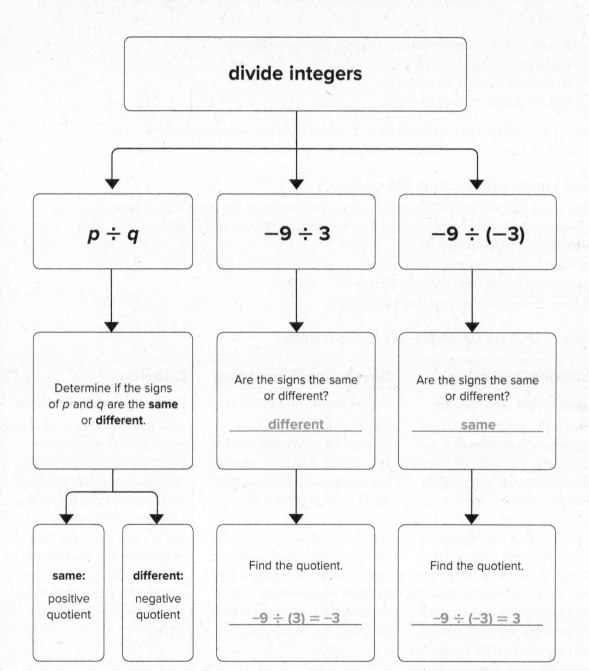

Lesson 5 Apply Integer Operations
English Learner Instructional Strategy

Sensory Support: Mnemonic Devices

Write *order of operations* on the board. Review the meaning of *order* and the mathematical meaning of *operations*. Ask students to list all the operations they can think of. Write their answers on the board. Introduce or review the correct order of operations and write them in a numbered list.

1) **P**arentheses or brackets (perform operations inside parentheses)
2) **E**xponents (evaluate the exponents)
3) **M**ultiply and **D**ivide (from left to right)
4) **A**dd and **S**ubtract (from left to right)

Point out that students can use the first letter of each (PEMDAS) to remember the correct order or operations. Have students add the order of operations to an anchor chart or word wall.

Math Language Routine: Three Reads

Ensure comprehension of the Check problem at the bottom of page 168 of the Student Book.
1st Read: Make sure students understand that *Fahrenheit* and *Celsius* are two different commonly-used temperature scales.
2nd Read: Support students in understanding that they are being asked to find the corresponding Celsius temperature for 32 degrees Fahrenheit.
3rd Read: Brainstorm ways to evaluate the formula.

English Language Development Leveled Activities

Entering/Emerging	Developing/Expanding	Bridging
Look, Listen, and Identify	**Signal Words and Phrases**	**Partners Work/Pairs Share**
Have students write each step in the order of operations on its own sticky note. Have students arrange the notes in order on their desks. Then have students check a partner's order to make sure it is correct. Discuss any differences. Teach the ordinal numbers *first, second, third,* and *fourth.* Introduce each word (and associate it with its corresponding cardinal number), say the word, and have students hold up the correct sticky note and repeat the word. Then ask, *What is the _____ step in the order of operations?* Students should hold up the corresponding sticky note.	Introduce or review words and phrases that signal order, such as *first, second, next, then, after that,* and *finally.* Have partners use the signal words or phrases in sentences that tell the correct order of operations. For example, they might write: **First, perform operations in parentheses. Then, evaluate the exponents. Next...** and so on. Ask volunteers to read their sentences to the group.	Have partners create a set of clues about order of operations. Encourage them to use words, phrases, and clauses that signal order. For example, **You do this after evaluating exponents from left to right. When you finish multiplying and dividing, you do this.** Have each pair trade clues with another pair who should use the clues to find the correct answer.

NAME _____ DATE _____ PERIOD _____

Lesson 5 Review Vocabulary
Apply Integer Operations

Use the definition map to list qualities about the vocabulary word or phrase.
Sample answers are given.

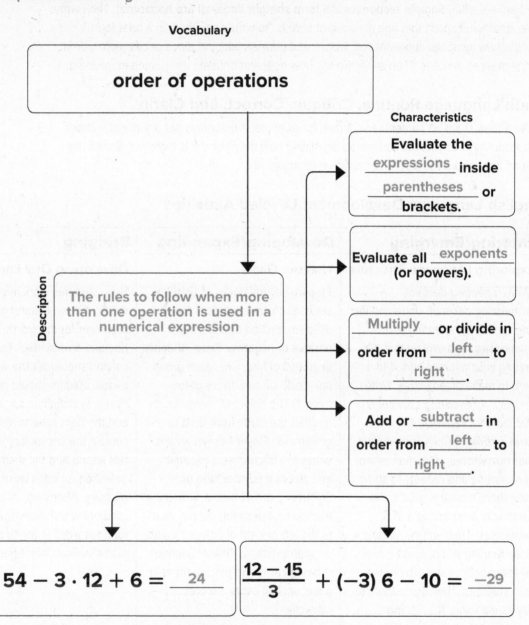

Vocabulary

order of operations

Characteristics

Evaluate the ___expressions___ inside ___parentheses___ or brackets.

Evaluate all ___exponents___ (or powers).

___Multiply___ or divide in order from ___left___ to ___right___.

Add or ___subtract___ in order from ___left___ to ___right___.

Description

The rules to follow when more than one operation is used in a numerical expression

$54 - 3 \cdot 12 + 6 = \underline{\;24\;}$

$\dfrac{12 - 15}{3} + (-3)\,6 - 10 = \underline{\;-29\;}$

Simplify each expression.

Lesson 1 Rational Numbers

English Learner Instructional Strategy

Sensory Support: Pictures and Photographs

Before the lesson, write *bar notation* and its Spanish cognate, *notación de barra* on a Word Wall and provide math examples. Show the bar notation symbol alongside other bars, such as the bar graph, parallel bars used in gymnastics, and a granola bar. Have students tell how all the bars are alike. **Sample responses: All form straight lines, all are horizontal.** Then write: *note, notation.* Explain that one meaning of *note* is "to write something in a brief form." Discuss how symbols, abbreviations, words, and phrases take the place of complete words and sentences in notes. Then show/discuss how *note* and *notation* are related in meaning.

Math Language Routine: Critique, Correct, and Clarify

Make a false claim for students to critique; for example, *A percent is not a rational number.* Ask students to correct the statement, explaining how they know it is incorrect. Revisit this routine throughout the lesson to provide reinforcement.

English Language Development Leveled Activities

Entering/Emerging	Developing/Expanding	Bridging
Exploring Language Structure Write: *repeating decimal, terminating decimal.* Underline the *-ing* ending in *repeating* and *terminating,* and explain that this ending is sometimes added to a verb to make an adjective. Write and say, *A **repeating** decimal is a decimal that **repeats**. A **terminating** decimal is a decimal that **terminates.*** Underline *repeat* in *repeating* and *repeats* to show they share a base word. Do the same with *terminating* and *terminates.* Then write: *swinging door, running water, singing bird, sleeping baby.* Say each phrase with students. Then guide them to say its meaning: **A ____ing ____ is a ____ that ____s.**	**Number Game** Prepare several decks of 12 index cards. Each card in a deck shows a different fraction that is either positive or negative. Place students in groups of four. Give each group one deck. Discuss these game rules: 1) The object of the game is to order the cards from least to greatest. 2) Player 1 draws a card, writes the fraction as a decimal, and places it number side up. 3) Player 2 draws a card, writes the fraction as a decimal and places it to the left or right of Player 1's card, as appropriate. 4) Players continue drawing cards and placing them in a line until all cards are ordered correctly.	**Developing Oral Language** Have students work in pairs to create a three-column graphic organizer for the words *repeating, bar,* and *terminating.* The left column should list the words, the middle column should contain an everyday definition for each word, and the right column should contain the vocabulary word from this lesson and the mathematical definition for each word from the glossary. Afterward, discuss as a group how the everyday definitions for each word relate to the mathematical definitions.

Multicultural Teacher Tip

In some countries, students may learn to read and write from right-to-left. As they learn English, they may struggle with the switch to left-to-right. The difficulty may carry over into math, with a student attempting to write and solve problems backward.

NAME _____ DATE _____ PERIOD _____

Lesson 1 Vocabulary
Rational Numbers

Use the vocabulary squares to write a definition, a sentence, and an example for each vocabulary word.   Sample answers are given.

	Definition
repeating decimal	the decimal form of a rational number

Example	Sentence
0.1666..., 2.75000...., $-0.\overline{3}$	The decimal form of the fraction $\frac{1}{9}$ is a repeating decimal.

	Definition
bar notation	in repeating decimals, the line or bar placed over the digits that repeat

Example	Sentence
$2.\overline{63}$, $1.\overline{18}$, $0.\overline{32}$	In the number $2.\overline{63}$, the bar notation indicates that the digits 63 repeat.

	Definition
terminating decimal	a repeating decimal which has a repeating digit of 0

Example	Sentence
0.25000..., 1.65, -0.825	Money values written in decimal form are terminating decimals.

Lesson 2 Add Rational Numbers

English Learner Instructional Strategy

Vocabulary Support: Activate Prior Knowledge

Introduce the word *inverse*. Write $3 + 4 = 7$ on the board. Have students say the number sentence. Then repeat for $7 - 4 = 3$. Point out that the starting point was 3. Then 4 was added, and then subtracted, to end up at the starting point again. Tell students that the word *inverse* means "opposite." Addition and subtraction are inverse operations.

Write the following on the board: *sum, difference, positive, negative, absolute value, number line*. Introduce or review the words. Then draw a number line on the board and have volunteers give examples of each term by drawing them on the line or explaining them using the number line. Have them plot $+\frac{1}{2}$ and $-\frac{1}{2}$ on the number line.

Point out how $+\frac{1}{2}$ and $-\frac{1}{2}$ are additive inverses. Write *additive inverse* on the board, say the word, and have students repeat. Underline *add* and point out that when additive inverses are added together, the sum is zero. Have students give other examples of additive inverses.

Math Language Routine: Discussion Supports

As students engage in discussing the Talk About It question on Student Book page 189, restate statements they make as a question to seek clarification and to confirm comprehension that it is sometimes more advantageous to write addends as fractions and other times as decimals. Encourage students to challenge each other's ideas when warranted.

English Language Development Leveled Activities

Entering/Emerging	Developing/Expanding	Bridging
Word Knowledge Write opposite on the board. Give a few simple examples of opposites, such as *happy/sad or bright/dark*. Have students give other examples. Then challenge students to give examples of number that are opposites. If they need assistance, write −3 on the board or on a number line. Ask, *What is the opposite?* Guide students to the idea that the number on the opposite side of zero that is the same distance from zero is the opposite. Write opposite *numbers = additive inverses*. Say the term and have students repeat.	**Developing Oral Language** Have partners ask and answer questions using sentence frames, such as **What is the additive inverse of ____? The additive inverse of ____ is ____. What is the opposite of ____? The opposite of ____ is ____. Give an example of additive inverses. ____ and ____ are additive inverses.**	**Share What You Know** Have students work with Emerging partners on the concept of additive inverses. Mentors should focus on making sure their partners understand the meaning of the term and the language for expressing their knowledge. Encourage mentors to offer sentence frames as students are able.

NAME _____ DATE _____ PERIOD _____

Lesson 2 Vocabulary
Add Rational Numbers

Use the definition map to list qualities about the vocabulary word or phrase.
Sample answers are given.

Vocabulary

> **additive inverse**

Description

> Two rational numbers that are opposites.

Characteristics

Two __rational numbers__ are opposites if they are represented by points that are on opposite sides of ___zero___ but the same ___distance___ from zero on a number line.

Integers, ___fractions___, and ___decimals___ can all have additive inverses.

The ___sum___ of a rational number and its additive inverse is ___zero___ .

−45.1	210	$-\dfrac{1}{10}$
45.1	−210	$\dfrac{1}{10}$

Find the additive inverse of each number.

Lesson 3 Subtract Rational Numbers
English Learner Instructional Strategy

Language Structure Support: Report Back

Introduce or review the terms *terminating decimal, non-terminating decimal,* and *simplest form.* Write the words on the board. Underline *terminating* and ask, *What does terminate mean?* Elicit "end." Then give an example of a terminating decimal, such as $\frac{3}{4} = .75$. Have students give other examples. Underline *non.* Ask, *What does non- mean?* Elicit "not." Say, *non-terminating decimal.* Point to the $\frac{3}{4} = .75$ example and ask, *Is this non-terminating?* no Then give an example of a non-terminating decimal: $\frac{1}{3} = .33333$. Have students give other examples. Introduce or review *simplest form.*

Write a number of fractions on the board, including some that have terminating or non-terminating decimals and some that are not in simplest form. For example: $\frac{1}{3}, \frac{4}{5}, \frac{12}{16}, \frac{15}{25}, \frac{17}{51},$ and so on. Have partners discuss and report back to you to describe the fraction.

The fraction _____ has a (non-)terminating decimal.
The fraction _____ [is/is not] in simplest form.

Math Language Routine: Stronger and Clearer Each Time

Have students individually think about their response to the Think About It question on page 200, then pair up with another student to refine and clarify their response through conversation. Students then revise their initial response and repeat with a new partner.

English Language Development Leveled Activities

Entering/Emerging	Developing/Expanding	Bridging
Look, Listen, and Identify Review terminating and non-terminating decimals and simplest form. Write two fractions (such as $\frac{3}{6}$ and $\frac{4}{9}$) on the board. Ask, *Which fraction is in simplest form.* Students should say or point to $\frac{4}{9}$. Ask, *Which fraction has a terminating decimal?* $\frac{3}{6}$ *Which has a non-terminating decimal?* $\frac{4}{9}$ Repeat for other fractions. As students are able, introduce simple sentences for them to practice: **_____ has a (non-)terminating decimal. _____ is in simplest form.**	**Round the Table** Organize students around a table. Every student should have a pencil. Give every other student a piece of paper. Have those students write any fraction at the top of the paper. Then have them pass the paper to their right. Their neighbor must use simple sentence frames to tell whether the fraction has a (non-) terminating decimal or is in simplest form. **The fraction _____ has a (non-) terminating decimal. It [is/is not] in simplest form.** The partner should verify that their neighbor is correct. If so, the neighbor writes another fraction on the paper and passes it to a new neighbor on the right.	**Share What You Know** Have students create a step-by-step process for putting a fraction into its simplest form. Then have students compare their lists with a partner. Monitor and provide feedback as necessary. Once students' processes are complete, have them teach a lesson to the whole group or to a small group of students who need a refresher.

NAME _____ DATE _____ PERIOD _____

Lesson 3 Vocabulary
Subtract Rational Numbers

Use the concept web to write pairs of rational numbers written in different forms and in the same form. Sample answers are given.

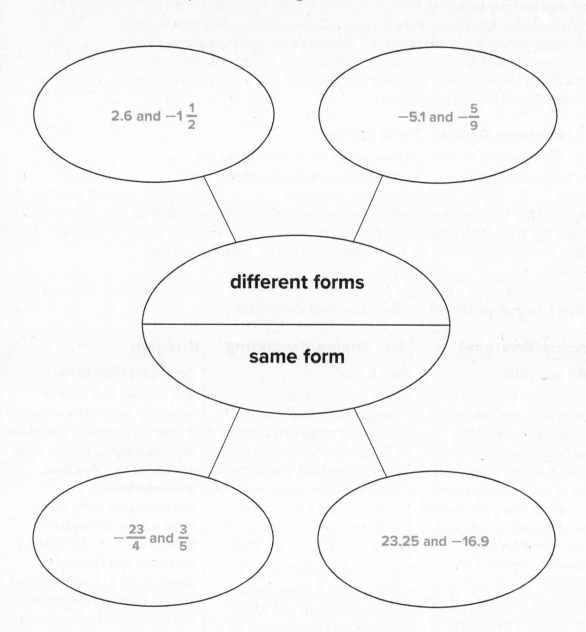

2.6 and $-1\frac{1}{2}$

-5.1 and $-\frac{5}{9}$

different forms

same form

$-\frac{23}{4}$ and $\frac{3}{5}$

23.25 and -16.9

Course 2 • Module 4 *Operations with Rational Numbers* **21**

Lesson 4 Multiply Rational Numbers

English Learner Instructional Strategy

Sensory Support: Illustrations, Diagrams, Drawings

At some point, students will be asked to write their own word problems. This may prove to be quite difficult for English learners, so the use of sentence frames such as the following will be helpful: **There are _____ athletes. _____ athletes play baseball. _____ of the athletes that play baseball also play basketball.** Tell students to use a whole number to fill in the first blank and fractions to fill in the remaining two blanks. Students may also have trouble solving word problems. Remind them that diagrams and drawings can be used to help solve a word problem. Have Entering/Emerging students who need help with sentence structures and terms used in the sentence frames (such as, *athletes, baseball,* and *basketball*) get help from a Developing/Expanding or Bridging student.

Math Language Routine: Three Reads

Ensure comprehension of the Check problem on page 210 of the Student Book.
1st Read: Make sure students understand that they are finding the depth of Lena's second dive.
2nd Read: Support students in understanding the meaning of the term *free diving* and that the second dive is two-fifths as deep as her first dive.
3rd Read: Brainstorm ways to first use estimation and then find the actual depth of the second dive.

English Language Development Leveled Activities

Entering/Emerging	Developing/Expanding	Bridging
Listen and Write	**Act It Out**	**Communication Guide**
Give students practice with rewriting word expressions as numerical expressions. Write: 1) one fourth of negative three eighths; 2) one half of three ninths; 3) one third of negative four fifths. First, read each item with students, helping them with pronunciation as needed. Then discuss this construction: *[fraction 1] of [fraction 2]*. Show students how finding fraction 1 of fraction 2 is the same as multiplying fraction 2 by fraction 1. Then have partners work together to rewrite and solve each expression. Check and discuss answers as a group.	Some students can better relate to fractional parts when they can visualize what they are calculating. Arrange with other teachers to allow your students to count the students in other classes on a given day. Then have your students work in groups to estimate how many of the students they counted would be represented by $\frac{1}{4}$, $\frac{1}{3}$, $\frac{1}{2}$, $\frac{2}{3}$, and so on. Have groups compare their work and discuss any difficulties they had with the calculations or differences they have discovered in their results.	Have students write rules for multiplying mixed numbers, using the following communication guide: **When multiplying, change mixed numbers to _____ fractions. (improper) Multiply the numerators and write the _____ in the numerator. (product) Multiply the _____ and write the denominator of the product. (denominators) Write the product in _____ form. (simplest)** When they have finished writing the rules, have them write an example problem and its solution. Ask them to share their work with a peer.

NAME _____ DATE _____ PERIOD _____

Lesson 4 Review Vocabulary
Multiply Rational Numbers

Use the flow chart to review the process for multiplying mixed numbers.
Sample answers are given.

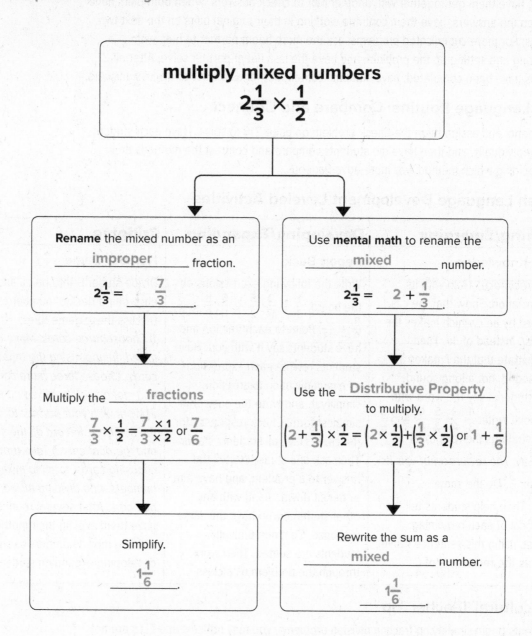

multiply mixed numbers
$$2\frac{1}{3} \times \frac{1}{2}$$

Rename the mixed number as an
_____ improper _____ fraction.
$$2\frac{1}{3} = \frac{7}{3}.$$

Use **mental math** to rename the
_____ mixed _____ number.
$$2\frac{1}{3} = 2 + \frac{1}{3}.$$

Multiply the _____ fractions _____.
$$\frac{7}{3} \times \frac{1}{2} = \frac{7 \times 1}{3 \times 2} \text{ or } \frac{7}{6}$$

Use the _____ Distributive Property _____
to multiply.
$$\left(2 + \frac{1}{3}\right) \times \frac{1}{2} = \left(2 \times \frac{1}{2}\right) + \left(\frac{1}{3} \times \frac{1}{2}\right) \text{ or } 1 + \frac{1}{6}$$

Simplify.
$$1\frac{1}{6}.$$

Rewrite the sum as a
_____ mixed _____ number.
$$1\frac{1}{6}.$$

Lesson 5 Divide Rational Numbers

English Learner Instructional Strategy

Collaborative Support: Partners Work/Pairs Check

Have partners work on problems you assign. Pair emerging students with expanding/bridging students. Have one partner complete the first problem while the second acts as coach. Then have partners switch roles for the second problem. When they have finished the second problem, have them get together with another pair to check answers. When both pairs have agreed on the answers, have them continue working in their original pairs on the next two problems. For more complicated problems, ask the more fluent partner to help with interpreting and setting up the problem, and have the less fluent partner solve. After all problems have been completed, have students come together as a class to discuss answers.

Math Language Routine: Compare and Connect

Pair students and assign them the Check problem on page 216 to solve. Have each student solve it individually, and then have the students compare and contrast the methods they used, deciding which method was more advantageous.

English Language Development Leveled Activities

Entering/Emerging	Developing/Expanding	Bridging
Word Knowledge	**Report Back**	**Number Game**
Write: *reciprocal*. Help with its pronunciation: Show that the *c* is followed by an *i*, which makes the *c* say /s/, instead of /k/. Then demonstrate that the *i* makes a short sound, not a long sound. Have students say the word with you. Next, write: $\frac{1}{3}, \frac{3}{14}, \frac{5}{2}, \frac{6}{11}$, and $\frac{8}{9}$. Show students the reciprocal of $\frac{1}{3}$. Say, *The reciprocal of* $\frac{1}{3}$ *is its reverse:* $\frac{3}{1}$. Do the same for $\frac{3}{14}$. Then help students tell the reciprocal of each remaining number, using this sentence frame: _____ **is the reciprocal of** _____.	Write the following expressions on the board: $\frac{1}{3} \div \frac{3}{14}, \frac{5}{2} \div \frac{6}{11}, \frac{8}{9} \div \frac{5}{2}, \frac{8}{9} \div \frac{2}{13}$. Point to each fraction and have students say it with you. Have students rewrite each expression as a multiplication expression, simplify it, and write the answer in simplest form. Check responses for the class. Have all students stand. Then ask one student to tell the answer to a problem, and have him or her sit down, along with any other students who have the same response. Continue until all students are seated. Then work through the problem as a class.	Divide students into pairs, and give each pair a deck of number cards. Discuss these game rules: *1) Choose three cards. Make a mixed number using the three cards. Choose three more cards and make another mixed number. 2) Work with your partner to divide the numbers. Record all the steps and the quotient. 3) Take turns choosing cards, forming mixed numbers, and dividing mixed numbers.* After several rounds, have them explain their method for dividing mixed numbers to an developing/expanding student.

Multicultural Teacher Tip

As students begin simplifying fraction division problems, you may notice some ELLs are not multiplying by the reciprocal of the divisor. In Mexico and Latin America, students are commonly taught to cross multiply when dividing fractions. The numerator of the first number is multiplied by the denominator of the second number to find the numerator of the answer, and vice versa for the denominator of the answer. For example, $\frac{1}{3} \div \frac{3}{4}$ is solved as $\frac{1 \times 4}{3 \times 3}$ to get $\frac{4}{9}$.

NAME _____ DATE _____ PERIOD _____

Lesson 5 Notetaking
Divide Rational Numbers

Use Cornell notes to better understand the lesson's concepts. Complete each
sentence by filling in the blanks with the correct word or phrase.

Questions	Notes
1. How do I divide fractions?	_____Multiply_____ by its multiplicative inverse, or _____reciprocal_____ .
2. How do I divide mixed numbers?	First, I rename the mixed number as a fraction greater than one, or an _____improper_____ fraction. Then I multiply the first fraction, by the _____reciprocal_____ of the second fraction.

Summary
How is dividing fractions related to multiplying? See students' work.
_____
_____
_____
_____
_____
_____
_____
_____

Lesson 6 Apply Rational Number Operations

English Learner Instructional Strategy

Language Structure Support: Cognates

Write the following words and their cognates on the board: *order of operations (orden de las operaciones, Commutative Property (propiedad commutativa), Associative Property (propiedad asociativa),* and *simplify (simplificar).* Introduce or review each term.

Then write an expression and have partners use order of operations to simplify it. You might use: $\frac{1}{2}\left(2+\frac{3}{3}\right)-\frac{5}{8}$. Once they are finished, ask questions to clarify that students understand the lesson vocabulary presented here. For example, *What is the first step?* **perform the operation in parentheses** Remind students to simplify their answer.

Point out cognates for math vocabulary whenever possible and have students add the words to an anchor chart or word wall.

Math Language Routine: Co-Craft Questions and Problems

Pair students and have them co-create a problem similar to the Check problem at the top of Student Book page 224. Have them work together to solve their problem and then trade their problem with another pair. After each pair solves the other pair's problems, have them form a group of four to check solutions and correct any mistakes that may have been made.

English Language Development Leveled Activities

Entering/Emerging	Developing/Expanding	Bridging
Listen and Identify	**Show What You Know**	**Communication Guides**
Review the order of operations using the PEMDAS mnemonic device. Write an expression on the board, such as $\frac{1}{2}\left(2+\frac{3}{4}\right)-\frac{5}{8}$. Ask, *What do we do first (next, after that, etc.)?* Allow one-word responses, such as **parentheses.** Say, *Yes, we add the numbers in parentheses.* Continue asking questions to guide students to simplify the expression.	Assign one of the following words to each student: *order of operations, Commutative Property, Associative Property, simplify.* Have them create their own definition of the word and then prepare a short presentation giving an example of the term. Encourage the audience to ask questions to the presenter. Once each presentation is complete, lead a short discussion to answer the question, *Why is [term] important?*	Have students write the steps for simplifying the expression $\frac{1}{2}\left(2+\frac{3}{4}\right)-\frac{5}{8}$. Then have them adjust their set of directions to include a few "mistakes." When they are done, have students trade with another student who should then review the list and make corrections. To encourage conversational language, write a few suggestions students can use to express themselves, such as, **Uh oh, I think I found a mistake. I don't think this one is correct. Should you ____ before doing this step? Let's go through this step together.**

NAME _____ DATE _____ PERIOD _____

Lesson 6 Review Vocabulary
Apply Rational Number Operations

Use the three-column chart to organize the vocabulary and key words in this lesson. Write the word in Spanish. Then complete the definition of each word.

English	Spanish	Definition
order of operations	orden de las operaciones	The _____rules_____ to follow when more than one _____operation_____ is used in a numerical expression
Associative Property	propiedad asociativa	The way in which numbers are grouped does not change the _____sum_____ or _____product_____ .
Commutative Property	propiedad commutativa	The _____order_____ in which two numbers are _____added_____ or _____multiplied_____ does not change the sum or product.
simplify	simplificar	Write an expression in simplest form

Lesson 1 Simplify Algebraic Expressions

English Learner Instructional Strategy

Vocabulary Support: Multiple-Meaning Words

Before the lesson, write *constant* and its Spanish cognate, *constant*. Introduce the words, and provide math examples. Utilize other translation tools for non-Spanish speaking ELLs. Add the words to a Word Wall. Then discuss noun and adjective meanings for the word, using real-world objects and demonstrations to support understanding.

Then write: *term*. Have students recall the meaning of *term*. **Each number in a sequence is a term.** Then say, *In math, a* **term** *can also be a* **part** *of an algebraic expression.* Tell students that terms do not contain addition or subtraction signs; they only contain numbers and/or variables and multiplication or division.

Math Language Routine: Collect and Display

As students discuss the question *How can algebra tiles be used to simplify an expression,* write key words and phrases you hear, such as *term, like terms, coefficient,* and *constant.* Display the words and phrases for student reference throughout the lesson. Update the collection with other relevant terms and new understandings as the lesson progresses.

English Language Development Leveled Activities

Entering/Emerging	Developing/Expanding	Bridging
Word Knowledge	**Developing Oral Language**	**Share What You Know**
Show how this lesson's vocabulary words are related using a word web. In the center circle, write: *term.* Say it with students, and help students to define it using their own words. Then around the center circle draw three smaller circles. In each, write one of the following words: *constant, coefficient, like terms.* Say each word with students. Connect its circle to the center circle to show that it is related to a term. Then invite volunteers to write examples of a constant, a coefficient, and like terms in the appropriate circle. Finally, help students define each word. Encourage students to use the word web as a reference.	Have students recall what *like fractions* are. **fractions with the same denominator** Then divide students into pairs. Have partners compare and contrast *like fractions* and *like terms.* Provide these sentence frames for them to use during their discussion: *Like fractions* and *like terms* are **similar because _____.** *Like fractions* and *like terms* are **different because like fractions have _____ and like terms have _____.**	Have Bridging students mentor Entering/Emerging and Developing/Expanding students on translating words into algebraic expressions, and vice versa, as follows: 1) Have each student write an algebraic expression. Then have them trade expressions and translate them into words. (Example: **4x + 13** says, **"Four times the variable x plus thirteen."**) Have the more fluent students help with translation and correct pronunciation as needed. 2) After completing several turns, the pairs should work backward, translating verbal expressions into algebraic expressions.

NAME _____ DATE _____ PERIOD _____

Lesson 1 Vocabulary
Simplify Algebraic Expressions

Use the vocabulary squares to write a definition, a sentence, and an example for each vocabulary word. Sample answers are given.

term	Definition a number, a variable, or a product or quotient of numbers and variables
Example $\frac{1}{5}$, 3x, 2, $\frac{y}{7}$	**Sentence** 5x and 3 are both terms in the expression 5x − 3.

like terms	Definition terms that contain the same variables raised to the same power
Example 3x and 9x, y^2 and $7y^2$	**Sentence** The terms 6a and 2a are like terms.

constant	Definition a term that does not contain a variable
Example 5, 7, 15	**Sentence** In the expression 3x + 5, the constant is 5.

Lesson 2 Add Linear Expressions

English Learner Instructional Strategy

Sensory Support: Illustrations, Diagrams, Drawings

Before the lesson, write *linear expression* and its Spanish cognate, *expresión lineal*. Introduce the words, and provide math examples. Utilize other translation tools for non-Spanish speaking ELLs. Add the terms to a Word Wall. Then write: *line/linear*. Underline *line* in both words, and tell students that *line* is the base word of *linear*. Then circle the *ar* in *linear* and tell students that this suffix means "resembling, or like." Help students create a definition for *linear* using its base word and suffix meaning. **resembling, or like, a line** Then draw a straight line, and discuss ways an expression might be like a line. Help students to think figuratively, guiding them to see that a line is *simple* and *direct*, as compared to shapes and squiggles.

Math Language Routine: Critique, Correct, and Clarify

Make a false claim for students to critique; for example, *The expression 10xy is a linear expression*. Ask students to correct the statement, explaining how they know it is incorrect. Revisit this routine throughout the lesson to provide reinforcement.

English Language Development Leveled Activities

Entering/Emerging	Developing/Expanding	Bridging
Word Knowledge	**Listen and Write**	**Turn and Talk**
To help students understand how to add linear expressions, use the concept of perimeter. Write and say the word *perimeter*. Then explain its meaning, "the distance around a shape's outer edge." Use a pointer to show the perimeters of classroom objects. Trace their outer edges and say, *This is the* **perimeter** *of the* _____. Next, briefly discuss how to measure the perimeter of an object. Then draw simple shapes, give measurements using a variable for their sides, and have students find their perimeter measurements. Have students say the measurements, using this sentence frame: **The perimeter is _____ inches.**	Repeat the Entering/Emerging Level activity. Then have partners create their own linear expression problem about the perimeter of a triangle. Discuss the following guidelines: *1) Draw a triangle. 2) Label the triangle with a measurement for each of its sides. Each measurement must include at least one term and one x variable.* After partners have drawn and labeled their shape, have them exchange papers with another pair and find the perimeter of the shape they received.	Ask students to turn and talk to a neighbor about ways that a linear expression is like a line. After students have had a few minutes to discuss, have them share their ideas with the class. Finally, have students discuss why the expression $x - 7$ is linear but the expression $x^4 - 7$ is not.

NAME _____ DATE _____ PERIOD _____

Lesson 2 Vocabulary
Add Linear Expressions

Use the definition map to list qualities about the vocabulary word or phrase.
Sample answers are given.

Vocabulary

linear expression

Characteristics of adding linear expressions

You can add linear expressions.

Description

an algebraic expression in which the variable is raised to the first power

Adding linear expressions is similar to simplifying expressions.

When adding, combine like terms.

$13x$

$\frac{1}{2}b + 5$

$7y - 6$

Examples of linear expressions

26 **Course 2 · Module 5** *Simplify Algebraic Expressions*

Lesson 3 Subtract Linear Expressions

English Learner Instructional Strategy

Vocabulary Support: Activate Prior Knowledge

Before the lesson, have students recall what they have learned about linear expressions. Write this on the board: $(-2x - 6) + (3x + 5) =$ _____. Then have students guide you through these steps toward its solution: 1) Use the Distributive Property. 2) Simplify. 3) Arrange the terms in columns of like terms. 4) Add like terms. After the class has solved the problem, have students tell you how to rework it using algebra tiles.

Then write: *additive inverse.* Remind students that they learned about additive inverses. Ask, *What is the **inverse** of something?* **its opposite** Then write these numbers: −3, 2, 5, −6. Have students tell each number's additive inverse. As needed, remind them that when a number is added to its additive inverse, the sum is zero.

Math Language Routine: Co-Craft Questions and Problems

Pair students and have them co-create a problem similar to the Apply problem on page 255 of the Student Book. Have them work together to solve their problem and then trade their problem with another pair. After each pair solves the other pair's problems, have them form a group of four to check solutions and correct any mistakes that may have been made. Revisit this routine throughout the lesson for reinforcement.

English Language Development Leveled Activities

Use the following problem with these leveled activities: *The number of customers in a store on the first day is represented by (6x − 3). The number of customers on the second day is represented by (x − 1). Write an expression to find how many more customers visited the store on the first day. Then evaluate the expression if x is equal to 50.*

Entering/Emerging	Developing/Expanding	Bridging
Modeled Talk	**Report Back**	**Partners Work/Pairs Check**
Work as a group to solve the problem. As each step is completed, tell what you did, emphasizing correct pronunciation, then have students repeat the key word. For example, say, *The **linear expression** is (6x − 3) − (x − 1).* Then have students chorally repeat: **linear expression**. Say, *The **additive inverse** of (x − 1) is (−x + 1).* Then have students chorally repeat: **additive inverse**. Continue in this way, modeling pronunciation for each step in the solving process.	Ask pairs to work through the problem together. Then have them report back to the class about how they solved their problem, using these sentence frames: **The linear expression is _____. The additive inverse of _____ is _____. If x equals 50, the there were _____ more customers on the first day.** Have the class check their solution to the problem.	Have partners work together to complete the problem. After they have solved it, have them write a couple sentences telling how they arrived at the solution. Then have them check answers with another pair of students. Students should use the sentences they wrote to justify their answer.

NAME _____ DATE _____ PERIOD _____

Lesson 3 Notetaking
Subtract Linear Expressions

Use Cornell notes to better understand the lesson's concepts. Complete each
sentence by filling in the blanks with the correct word or phrase.

Questions	Notes
1. How do I subtract linear expressions?	I subtract _____ like _____ terms. I use _____ zero _____ pairs if needed.
2. What is the additive inverse of a linear expression?	The additive inverse of a linear expression is an expression with terms that are _____ opposites _____. The sum of a linear expression and its additive inverse is _____ zero _____.

Summary

How can I use the additive inverse to help you subtract linear expressions?

See students' work.

_____

_____

_____

_____

_____

_____

_____

_____

Course 2 · Module 5 *Simplify Algebraic Expressions* **27**

Lesson 4 Factor Linear Expressions
English Learner Instructional Strategy

Vocabulary Support: Build Background Knowledge

Write *monomial* and *factored form* and their Spanish cognates, *monomio* and *forma factorizada,* respectively on a Word Wall. Introduce the words, and provide math examples to support understanding. Underline *mono* in *monomial,* and explain this root word means "one." Write a few examples of monomials and non-monomials on the board for visual support. Point out that the "Monomial" examples have only *one* term each, while the "Not Monomial" examples have two or more terms. Discuss other words with this root, such as *monotone, monologue,* and *monopoly.*

Math Language Routine: Information Gap

Have pairs of students play *What's the GCF?*. Student *A* writes a monomial on a card; Student *B* writes a monomial on a different card. Students exchange cards and individually determine the GCF of the two monomials. Encourage students to challenge each other's answers and to refine or clarify their findings through conversation.

English Language Development Leveled Activities

Entering/Emerging	Developing/Expanding	Bridging
Word Knowledge	**Anchor Chart**	**Partners Work/Pairs Check**
Write: $2 \cdot 2 \cdot 5 = 20$ and *factored form.* Underline *factor.* Point to 2 and ask, *Is 2 a factor?* **yes** Repeat with 5. Help students define *factor.* Then circle the *ed* in *factored.* Explain that sometimes the *-ed* ending is used to make a noun into an adjective, which is a describing word. Show and explain how *factored* describes *form:* The *factored form* of an expression is the *form* that shows its *factors.* Finally, write expressions in both their factored and unfactored forms. Ask, *Which is the factored form?* Students point to the answer.	Draw a four-column chart on the board, with these column heads: Factor (noun), Factor (verb), Factored Form, Greatest Common Factor. Then, under each head, have students help you write the following: 1) a math definition for the term, using students' words; 2) a sentence that uses the term in context; and 3) a math example. The following are sample responses for the noun *factor*: **1) Definition: a number or variable multiplied by another number or variable to form a product; 2) One factor of 21 is 7; 3) Factors of 21 are 1, 3, 7, 21.**	Have partners work together to write word problems involving monomials. Tell them their word problems must include information that can be represented in a linear expression and a solution that involves factoring the expression. Then have students trade their problems with another pair and solve the word problem they receive. Finally, have partners check answers with the pair who wrote the problem.

Multicultural Teacher Tip

You may see some ELLs using a method other than the factor trees commonly used in U.S. classrooms to find factors. In Mexico, students are taught to draw a vertical line. On the left side, they write the number to be factored, and then the first prime factor is written on the right side. The number divided by the factor is then written on the left side, below the original number, and the process continues. In factoring 18, for example, the result would be *18, 9, 3, 1* listed on the left side, and the prime factors *2, 3, 3* listed on the right.

18	2
9	3
3	3
1	

NAME _____ DATE _____ PERIOD _____

Lesson 4 Vocabulary
Factor Linear Expressions

Use the vocabulary squares to write a definition, a sentence, and an example for each vocabulary word. Sample answers are given.

monomial	Definition
	a number, variable, or product of a number and one or more variables
Example	**Sentence**
$13x$, -9, 27, y	A monomial contains only one term.

factor (verb)	Definition
	to write an expression as a product of its factors
Example	**Sentence**
$3x = 3 \cdot x$	We can factor the expression $10b$ as $10 \cdot b$.

factored form	Definition
	an expression written as the product of its factors
Example	**Sentence**
$27b + 3c = 3(9b + c)$	The factored form of $5y + 10$ is $5(y + 2)$.

Lesson 5 Simplify Algebraic Expressions

English Learner Instructional Strategy

Vocabulary Support: Math Word Wall

Create a class word wall to review all the vocabulary in this module. Assign one or two of the following words to each pair of students: *terms, like terms, coefficient, constant, simplest form, linear expression, additive inverse, factor, factored form greatest common factor, monomial, distributive property, and simplify.* Have them work together to write the word, its cognate (if applicable), a definition, and an example. Before adding the information to the word wall, ask a volunteer from each pair to present the information to the class. Clear up any mistakes or misunderstandings (either with language or with the math content), and then have students add the information to the wall.

Math Language Routine: Discussion Supports

As students engage in discussing the Talk About It questions on Student Book page 267, restate statements they make as a question to seek clarification and to confirm comprehension, providing validation or correction when necessary. Encourage students to challenge each other's ideas when warranted, as well as to elaborate on their ideas and give examples.

English Language Development Leveled Activities

Entering/Emerging	Developing/Expanding	Bridging
Look, Listen, and Identify	**Signal Words and Phrases**	**Building Oral Language**
Review the following terms and write them on the board: *combine like terms, factored form, distributive property.* Write a linear expression, such as $4(5 - x) - x$. Point to the expression and ask, *What is this?* **linear expression** Say, *We are going to simplify this expression.* Have students use one of the terms to answer your questions: *What do we do first?* **distributive property** *What do we do next?* **combine like terms** Repeat for other expressions.	Write a linear expression, such as $4(5 - x) - x$. Introduce or review words and phrases that signal order, such as *first, second, next, then, after that,* and *finally.* Have partners discuss how to simplify the expression and then use the signal words or phrases in sentences that tell the correct order for simplifying the expression.	Review how to produce complex sentences. Remind students that a complex sentence has one independent clause (which can stand alone as a sentence) and at least one dependent clause (which cannot stand alone). Select one construction, write a sentence frame for it, and have students practice it. For example, **After you have _____, you should _____.** (Remind students that a verb with -ed will fill the first blank.) Other possibilities include: **Once you are finished _____ing, _____. Before you _____, you should _____.**

NAME _____ DATE _____ PERIOD _____

Module 5 Review Vocabulary
Combine Operations with Linear Expressions

Complete the four-square chart to review the multiple-meaning word or phrase.
Sample answers are given.

Everyday Use to make something easier to understand or easier to do The Internet has helped simplify the research process.	**Math use in a sentence** When I simplify the expression $3x + 5y + (-2y) - 5(2x)$, I get the answer $-7x + 3y$.
Math Use to write an expression in a simpler way by combining like terms and eliminating parentheses Simplify the expression $3x + 5y + (-2y) - 5(2x)$.	**Example from this lesson** Simplify $-2(x + 3) + 8x$ $-2(x + 3) + 8x = -2x - 6 + 8x$ $= 6x - 6$

simplify

Lesson 1 Write and Solve One-Step Equations

English Learner Instructional Strategy

Vocabulary Support: Cognates

Before the lesson, review *equation, solution,* and *equivalent equation* and their Spanish cognates, *ecuación, solución, ecuación equivalente,* respectively. Introduce the words, provide realia to support understanding, and add the words to a Word Wall. Utilize other appropriate translation tools for non-Spanish speaking ELLs. Then write and say: *equal, equality, equation, equivalent.* Point out common letters among the words, and discuss how the meanings of these terms are related. Encourage students to write the terms in their math notebooks, along with notes, pictures, and examples that help them recall the terms' definitions.

Finally, write and say: coefficient. Define the word and provide a math example. Then underline the *co-* prefix and tell students it means "together." Discuss how a coefficient and variable work together in an equation. Then write: $7x$, $2y$, $5t$, $8z$. Point to each expression and have students name its parts using these sentence frames: **The coefficient is _____. The variable is _____.** Finally, invite students to name other words they know that begin with the prefix co- (such as, **coexist, cooperate, copilot**).

Math Language Routine: Information Gap

Have pairs of students play *Complete the Equation.* Give Student *A* a card with an incomplete one-step equation, such as $x + \_\_ = 52$. Give Student *B* a different card with a solution, such as 27. Student *A* asks for the solution and then completes the equation, $x + 25 = 52$. Students then switch roles. Encourage students to challenge each other's answers when warranted.

English Language Development Leveled Activities

Entering/Beginning	Developing/Expanding	Bridging/Reteaching
Listen and Identify The *th* digraph can be very difficult for many ELL students. To illustrate the pronunciation of /th/, demonstrate proper tongue placement between your teeth. Then hold a piece of paper in front of your mouth as you blow out through your teeth, saying /thththth/. Have students practice. Next write: $0.25n$, $-\frac{3}{4}x$, $-\frac{7}{9}d$, $1.6k$. **The [decimal/fraction] coefficient is _____. The variable is _____.** Then go over responses as a class. Point to each expression and say its parts aloud. Then have students repeat chorally. Remind them to take care in pronouncing the /th/ ending on fraction names.	**Sentence Frames** Write the equation $\frac{3}{4}x = 1$. Ask, What is the coefficient? $\frac{3}{4}$ What kind of coefficient is $\frac{3}{4}$? **a fraction coefficient** Then say, Let's solve the equation. One rule says that a fraction multiplied by its **inverse** equals 1. How can we write a fraction that is the **inverse** of $\frac{3}{4}$? Have students respond: **Make the numerator _____ and the denominator _____.** Multiply $\frac{3}{4}$ by $\frac{4}{3}$ to get $\frac{12}{12}$ or 1. Then write $\frac{2}{3}$, $\frac{3}{5}$, $\frac{4}{9}$. Have students say each fraction and its inverse. Remind them that a multiplicative inverse is also called a *reciprocal*.	**Share What You Know** After students have worked through several problems involving equations with rational coefficients, have partners choose a problem and make a plan for presenting how they found the solution. Tell them to compare answers to the problem to ensure their answers agree. Then have pairs work together to write guidelines for solving the problem. Once pairs have finished, have them present their problem to the class, explaining how they arrived at its solution.

NAME _____ DATE _____ PERIOD _____

Lesson 1 Vocabulary

Write and Solve One-Step Equations

Use the three-column chart to organize the vocabulary in this lesson. Write the word in Spanish. Then write the definition of each word. Sample answers are given.

English	Spanish	Definition
equation	ecuación	a mathematical sentence that contains an equals sign, =, stating that two quantities are equal
solution	solución	a replacement value for the variable in an open sentence; a value for the variable that makes an equation true
equivalent equations	ecuaciones equivalentes	two or more equations with the same solution
coefficient	coeficiente	the numerical factor of a term that contains a variable
rational coefficient	coeficiente racionales	the rational factor of a term that contains a variable

Lesson 2 Solve Two-Step Equations: $px + q = r$
English Learner Instructional Strategy

Vocabulary Support: Anchor Chart

Before the lesson, create an anchor chart titled *Order of Operations* and list the order of operations. Then write this example on the chart: $3 \cdot 4 + 2$. Point to $3 \cdot 4 + 2$ and say, *This expression has two* **operations**. *What are they?* Point to the multiplication symbol and prompt students to say: **multiply**. Then point to the addition sign and prompt students to say: **add**. Next say, *We will simplify this expression in* **two steps**. *Each operation is* **one step**. Explain that you will use the Order of Operations to decide which operation to do first and which to do second. On the chart, find multiply or divide. Then find add or subtract. Ensure students know to read the equation from left to right. Then point to your example and ask, *Which operation do we do* **first***?* **multiply** Ask students for the answer to $3 \cdot 4$. **12** Write it under the example. Then ask, *Which operation do we do* **second***?* **add** Show students that you take the product from the first operation and add it in the second operation. Ask students for the simplified form: **14**.

Math Language Routine: Critique, Correct, and Clarify

Create other two-step equations like the one in Example 3 on page 291. Make correct and incorrect statements about the steps in solving the equation; for example, *The first step to solve this equation is to use the Division Property of Equality. Am I correct?* Students critique, correct and clarify explaining how they know it's a correct or incorrect statement. Revisit this routine throughout the lesson to provide reinforcement.

English Language Development Leveled Activities

Entering/Emerging	Developing/Expanding	Bridging
Word Knowledge	**Communication Guide**	**Show What You Know**
Write: $3t - 7 = 14$. Ask students to name each operation in the equation: **multiply, subtract**. Next say, *Let's solve the equation.* Write and say, *undo*. Underline the prefix *un-*, and explain that it means "opposite." Show students how to "do the opposite" in order to solve the equation. Read aloud the order of operations. Then ask, *How can we* **undo** *the order of steps?* Have students respond using these sentence frames: **First, _____. (add, subtract) Second, _____. (multiply, divide)** Next, point to each operation in the equation and ask, *How do I* **undo** *multiplication?* **divide** *How do I* **undo** *subtraction?* **add** Then solve the equation.	Give students several two-step equations, such as $3t - 7 = 14$. Encourage them to write which operations are shown in the equation. Then ask them to tell how to "undo" the operations in the equation. Have students use this communication guide to form their responses: **The equation _____, shows two operations: _____ and _____. To undo it, I will _____ first. Then I will _____. The solution is _____.** After students have had time to work, discuss each equation as a class. Invite volunteers to share their responses.	Have students tell how solving two-step operations is similar to solving one-step operations. Then have them tell how it is different. Provide these sentence frames to help students form their responses: **Solving a two-step operation is like solving a one-step operation because _____. (Sample response: I have to undo both operations.) Solving a two-step operation is different from solving a one-step operation because _____. (Sample response: I have to undo two-step operations in a certain order.)** Have students discuss their response with a partner.

NAME _____ DATE _____ PERIOD _____

Lesson 2 Vocabulary
Solve Two-Step Equations: px + q = r

Use the definition map to list qualities about the vocabulary word or phrase.
Sample answers are given.

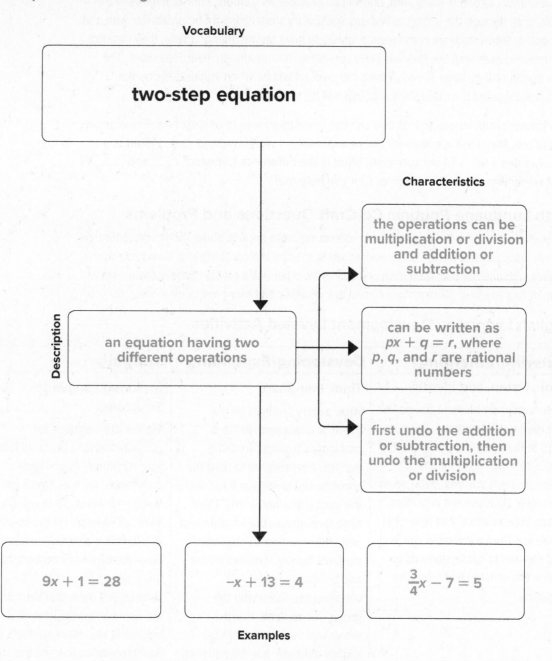

Vocabulary

two-step equation

Description

an equation having two different operations

Characteristics

the operations can be multiplication or division and addition or subtraction

can be written as $px + q = r$, where p, q, and r are rational numbers

first undo the addition or subtraction, then undo the multiplication or division

Examples

$9x + 1 = 28$

$-x + 13 = 4$

$\frac{3}{4}x - 7 = 5$

Course 2 · Module 6 *Write and Solve Equations* **31**

Lesson 3 Write and Solve Two-Step Equations:
$px + q = r$
English Learner Instructional Strategy

Language Structure Support: Communication Guides

Review the terms *add, subtract, multiply, divide, equation, coefficient, constant,* and *variable.* Ask volunteers to define each term, offering an example as support. Prior to beginning the lesson, scan through the lesson to find any vocabulary students might be unfamiliar with and preteach it. When students come upon a word you have taught ahead of time, they may not remember its meaning, but they will likely remember having already heard the word. The more exposure they have ahead of time, the easier it will be when students encounter difficult words, and the more likely students will be to ask for help.

Help students with language that they can use when they need to request help. For example, **Excuse me. May I ask a question? I have a question. I wonder about _____. What is a _____? Is this a _____? I am confused. What is the difference between _____ and _____? I can't remember what _____ means. Can you help me?**

Math Language Routine: Co-Craft Questions and Problems

Pair students and have them co-create a problem similar to the one about Diego's aquarium on Student Book page 301. Have them work together to solve their problem and then trade their problem with another pair. After each pair solves the other pair's problems, have them form a group of four to check solutions and correct any mistakes that may have been made.

English Language Development Leveled Activities

Entering/Emerging	Developing/Expanding	Bridging
Look, Listen, and Identify	**Think-Pair-Share**	**Exploring Language Structure**
Write a story problem on the board and read it with students. For each word in the problem, point to it and ask, *Is this an important word?* When students say **yes**, write down the word. Then use the important words in a sentence that tells what is known. Then use simple words and phrases to guide students to define the variable and write the equation.	Write a story problem on the board or direct students to a problem or example from the module. Ask students to read the problem and identify and list only the most important words. Then have them define the variable and write the equation. Finally, have students turn to another student and compare results. Ask volunteers to share with the group. Tell students that the words and variables might be slightly different, but the equation should be the same.	Review the language for commands. Have students follow your directions as you give commands, such as *Stand up. Raise your hand. Sit down. Smile.* Write an example on the board. Ask, *Is this a complete sentence?* Students might say **no** because there does not appear to be a subject. Tell them that since these are commands, the implied subject is *You.* Have students use this information to write the steps for writing and solving a two-step equation as though they were giving commands to another person. Then have them say the commands.

NAME _____ DATE _____ PERIOD _____

Lesson 3 Review Vocabulary

Write and Solve Two-Step Equations: $px + q = r$

Complete the four-square chart to review the multiple meaning word or phrase.
Sample answers are given.

Everyday Use	Math use in a sentence
not always the same; likely to change	When I write an expression, I can use the letter x as a variable in the place of a number I don't know.
The weather in Indiana is variable. It can change a lot from day to day.	

variable

Math Use	Example from this lesson
a symbol, usually a letter, used to represent a number in a mathematical expression or sentence	Toya had her birthday party at the movies. It cost $27 for pizza and $8.50 per friend for the movie tickets. Write and solve an equation to determine how many friends Toya had at her party if she spent $78.

Lesson 4 Solve Two-Step Equations: $p(x + q) = r$
English Learner Instructional Strategy

Language Structure Support: Frontload Vocabulary

During the lesson, have students work with a bilingual peer or mentor to solve the problems. Before assigning the problems, define any unknown words using real-world objects, illustrations, and demonstrations to support understanding.

Math Language Routine: Collect and Display

As students discuss how to use algebra tiles to solve two-step equations, write the methods you hear, such as *drawing a bar diagram, writing an equation, working backward*. Elicit and include examples of each method. Display the methods for student reference throughout the lesson. Update the collection with other relevant terms, methods, and new understandings as the lesson progresses.

English Language Development Leveled Activities

Entering/Emerging	Developing/Expanding	Bridging
Word Identification	**Turn and Talk**	**Round the Table**
Write the following equations on the board: $\frac{2}{3}(n - 15) = 16$; $4(m + 3) = 8$; $1.6(p - 2) = 8.2$. Then write: *factor, decimal coefficient, fraction coefficient, product.* Have students copy each equation into their math notebooks. Then have them label each part of the equations using the terms on the board. After they have had time to work, call on volunteers to share answers. Model pronunciations, as needed. In particular, help students note that the *ci* in *decimal* is pronounced /si/, the *cient* in *coefficient* is pronounced /shənt/, and the *-tion* in *fraction* is pronounced /shən/.	Write the following two-step equation on the board: $0.3(t - 2) = 0.6$. Have students first solve the equation independently. Then have them turn to a neighbor and explain their solution using this communication guide: **First, I divided ____ and ____ by ____. Next, I simplified ____ and ____. The solution is $t =$ ____.** Finally, ask a volunteer to name the kind of coefficient used in this problem. **decimal coefficient**	Divide students into three groups. Have groups write a word problem based on this equation: $4(x + 2) = 32$. Then have students pass their word problem to another group. Tell groups to solve the word problem they received using a bar graph to illustrate the solution. Then ask students to trade again, this time passing the word problem to the only group that hasn't seen it yet. Have the third group draw two mats with algebra tiles to illustrate the solution. Finally, ask students to return their word problem to the group that wrote it. Have the original writers check both word problem solutions to see if they agree. If they do not, have students find the error(s).

NAME _____ DATE _____ PERIOD _____

Lesson 4 Review Vocabulary

Solve Two-Step Equations: $p(x + q) = r$

Use the concept web to write and solve examples of two-step equations. Include examples written in the forms $px + q = r$ and $p(x + q) = r$. Sample answers are given.

$-x + 14 = 6$

$x = 8$

$\dfrac{2}{5}x - 9 = -3$

$x = 15$

two-step equations

$-7(5x - 3) = -49$

$x = 2$

$3(2x + 4) = 72$

$x = 10$

Course 2 · Module 6 *Write and Solve Equations* **33**

Lesson 5 Write and Solve Two-Step Equations:
$p(x + q) = r$
English Learner Instructional Strategy

Collaborative Support: Show What You Know

Organize students into four groups of varying levels of English proficiency. Assign a problem to each group and have them work out the problem together. Then have them describe to each other the steps they performed to write and solve the equation. Finally, for each problem/group, have a student from the group come forward and perform the first step while explaining what they are doing. For example: **I am describing the problem, using only the most important words**. Allow Entering/Emerging students to just do the math or describe the step with a single word or short phrase, such as **multiply**.

Math Language Routine: Three Reads

Ensure comprehension of the Check problem on page 319 of the Student Book.
1st Read: Make sure students understand that they are being asked to determine how many yards of red fabric is needed to make the five costumes. Ensure comprehension of the meaning of *fabric* and *costumes*.
2nd Read: Focus students' attention on the total amount of fabric that will be used and how much blue fabric is required for each costume.
3rd Read: See if students have any questions about the situation before working on solving the problem.

English Language Development Leveled Activities

Entering/Emerging	Developing/Expanding	Bridging
Building Oral Language	**Exploring Language Structure**	**Partners Work/Pairs Share**
Write $3(x + 7) = -9$ on a large sheet of paper. Organize students into two groups. Give one group an algebra mat and algebra tiles. Give the other group the paper with the equation. Direct the first group to solve the equation for x using manipulatives. Display the following sentence frames: **Add ____. Subtract ____. Multiply by ____. Divide by ____.** As the first group completes each step using the tiles, have them guide the second group in solving the equation on paper. $x = -10$ Write a new equation and have groups switch roles.	Assign a problem to student pairs. Have one student guide the other in solving the problem step-by-step. Display the following sentence frames: **Add ____. Subtract ____. Multiply by ____. Divide by ____.** Circulate and listen to students to be sure they are using the present tense. Then have the second student describe the steps they completed using the past tense. **I added ____. I subtracted ____. I multiplied by ____. I divided by ____.** Assign a different problem and have students switch roles.	Have partners collaborate to come up with a real-world scenario that would translate into a two-step equation. Monitor and offer feedback as students write out their scenarios. On a separate piece of paper, partners should write the equation and solution to their scenario. Ask partners to trade scenarios with another team who will write and solve the equation. Finally, have pairs come together and discuss each scenario, its equation, and the solution. Does everyone agree?

Lesson 5 Notetaking

Write and Solve Two-Step Equations: $p(x + q) = r$

Use Cornell notes to better understand the lesson's concepts. Complete each
sentence by filling in the blanks with the correct word or number.

Questions	Notes
1. How can I use a bar diagram to solve $4(x + 5) = 28$?	Use a __bar diagram__ to help solve the equation: $\vdash - - - - - - - \boxed{28} - - - - - - - - \dashv$ $\boxed{(x+5)}\ \boxed{(x+5)}\ \boxed{(x+5)}\ \boxed{(x+5)}$ From the diagram, I can tell that one-fourth of 28 is equal to __$(x + 5)$__. So, I can solve for x: $\dfrac{28}{\underline{4}} = \dfrac{4(x+5)}{4}$ ___Division___ Property of Equality $\underline{7} = x + 5$ Simplify $\underline{7} - 5 = x + 5 - \underline{5}$ ___Subtraction___ Property of Equality $\underline{2} = x$ Simplify
2. How can I use the Properties of Equality to solve $4(x + 5) = 28$?	$4(x + 5) = 28$ $4(\underline{x}) + 4(\underline{5}) = 28$ Expand using the ___Distributive___ Property $4x + \underline{20} = 28$ Simplify $4x + \underline{20} - \underline{20} = 28 - \underline{20}$ ___Subtraction___ Property of Equality $4x = 8$ Simplify $\dfrac{4x}{4} = \dfrac{8}{4}$ Division Property of Equality $x = 2$

Summary

Do you prefer using a bar diagram or the Properties of Equality to solve
equations? Explain. **See students' work.**

_____

_____

_____

Lesson 1 Solve One-Step Addition and Subtraction Inequalities

English Learner Instructional Strategy

Collaborative Support: Act It Out

Use a real-world of example of mailing a letter to help students understand comparing numbers. Tell students a first class stamp is used to send letters that weigh 1 ounce or less. Have students prepare a post office skit with a partner. One student is the customer and the other is the postal worker. The customer can bring a letter or package to the postal worker and ask for help with sending it. **I want to send this [letter/package] first class. How much will it cost?** The postal worker can weigh the letter or package and then advise the customer. **The letter weighs less than 1 ounce. You can buy a first class stamp for 50 cents. The package weighs more than 1 ounce. You will need a special stamp.**

Math Language Routine: Compare and Connect

Pair students and have them work on the Check problem on page 333 of the Student Book. Have them compare and contrast the processes of solving equations with solving inequalities. Restate statements they make as a question to seek clarification.

English Language Development Leveled Activities

Entering/Emerging	Developing/Expanding	Bridging
Choral Responses	Building Oral Language	Show What You Know
Help students understand what a *true* statement is. Display cards showing different colors. Write and say the colors' names. Then show students objects from the classroom. Make statements about the colors of the objects. For example, hold up a yellow pencil and say, *The pencil is yellow. This statement is* **true**. Then hold up a red apple and say, *The apple is green. This statement is* **not true**. Repeat with other objects and have students say **true** or **not true** to describe the statement. Then write: $5 > 3; 4 > 6; 7 < 3; 2 < 9$. Have students copy the *true* statements on their paper.	Write the following inequalities on the board: $w + 4 < 11$; $x - 2 > 3$; $y - 5 \leq 14$; $z + 3 \geq 5$. Ask students to solve each inequality. Then have them explain their solutions to a neighbor using these sentence frames: **If** _____ **is [greater than/less than]** _____, **then** _____ **[plus/minus]** _____ **is [greater/less] than** _____ **[plus/minus]** _____. Tell students to take turns explaining their solutions. If their solutions are not the same, have the two students rework the inequality together until they can agree on a solution.	Have partners work together to prepare a list of inequality expressions, in symbols and words. For example: $a < b$: *a is less than b, a is fewer than b* $a > b$: *a is greater than b, a is more than b* $a \leq b$: *a is less than or equal to b, a is no more than b, a is at most b* $a \geq b$: *a is greater than or equal to b, a is at least b, a is no less than b*

Multicultural Teacher Tip

ELLs who are familiar with the angle symbol at the front of an angle designation may be confused by inequality symbols. They may have trouble distinguishing between the two signs, so emphasize the difference prior to beginning the lesson.

NAME _____ DATE _____ PERIOD _____

Lesson 1 Vocabulary
Solve One-Step Addition and Subtraction Inequalities

Use the vocabulary squares to write a definition, a sentence, and an example for
each vocabulary word.   Sample answers are given.

inequality	**Definition** an open sentence that uses $<$, $>$, $\neq$, $\leq$, or $\geq$ to compare two quantities
Example $3x > 5$	**Sentence** The inequality $3x > 5$ is read as three times x is greater than five.

Subtraction Property of Inequality	**Definition** If you subtract the same number from each side of an inequality, the inequality remains true.
Example $5 + a > 15$ $5 + a - 5 > 15 - 5$ $a > 10$	**Sentence** You can use the Subtraction Property of Inequality to solve the inequality $5 + a > 15$. Subtract 5 from each side and simplify to $a > 10$.

Addition Property of Inequality	**Definition** If you add the same number to each side of an inequality, the inequality remains true.
Example $b - 7 \leq 10$ $b - 7 + 7 \leq 10 + 7$ $b \leq 17$	**Sentence** You can use the Addition Property of Inequality to solve the inequality $b - 7 \leq 10$. Add 7 to each side and simplify to $b \leq 17$.

Course 2 · **Module 7** *Write and Solve Inequalities*   **35**

Lesson 2 Write and Solve One-Step Addition and Subtraction Inequalities

English Learner Instructional Strategy

Graphic Support: Signal Word Chart

Tell students that there are words in problems that signal inequalities. Write the following list of words and phrases on the board: *over, less than, at least, at most, more than, under, below, above, no more than, no less than, up to*. Have students highlight any of these words or phrases they see in the problems.

Have students create a four-column chart in their math notebooks using *greater than* ($>$), *less than* ($<$), *greater than or equal to* ($\geq$), and *less than or equal to* ($\leq$) as column headings. Have partners work together to determine which word or phrase signals which inequality and write it in the appropriate column. Clarify meanings with examples, if necessary.

Math Language Routine: Co-Craft Questions and Problems

Pair students and have them co-create a problem similar to the Check problem on Student Book page 343. Have them work together to solve their problem and then trade their problem with another pair. After each pair solves the other pair's problems, have them form a group of four to check solutions and correct any mistakes that may have been made. Revisit this routine throughout the lesson for reinforcement.

English Language Development Leveled Activities

Entering/Emerging	Developing/Expanding	Bridging
Look, Listen, and Identify	**Look, Say, and Write**	**Share What You Know**
Graph several inequalities on number lines. Copy and distribute to each pair of students. Guide students as they try to determine the inequality represented on the graph by asking simple questions and giving simple directions. For example, say, *Where does the graph begin? Point to that place.* Students point. Ask, *What number is it? Is the graph shaded to the left or right? Is the inequality greater or less than? Is the dot open or closed? So, is the inequality [greater/less] than or equal to?* Remember that students may only be able to point or say **yes** or **no**.	Graph several inequalities on number lines. Copy and distribute to each pair of students. Have students write an inequality based on the graph. Encourage students to use the following language as they work: **The dot is open. the number is not equal to _____. It is shaded to the [left/right] of _____. This means we use [greater/less] than. The inequality is _____.** Have students write the inequality mathematically and in words.	Partner a Bridging student with an Entering/Emerging or Developing/Expanding student and have them browse the lesson's story problems and identify any troublesome vocabulary. The Bridging student should help the partner determine the meanings of any unknown words by using gestures, pictures, dictionaries, or short phrases as an explanation.

NAME _____ DATE _____ PERIOD _____

Lesson 2 Vocabulary

Write and Solve One-Step Addition and Subtraction Inequalities

Draw a line to connect *inverse operations* to each correct definition or example.

$$5 \cdot 9 = 9 \cdot 5$$

$$\frac{2}{3}a > 5$$
$$\frac{2}{3}a \cdot \frac{3}{2} > 5 \cdot \frac{3}{2}$$

Two operations that have the same result, such as multiplication and repeated addition.

inverse operations

$$4(b - 9) = 16b$$
$$\frac{4(b - 9)}{4} = \frac{16b}{4}$$

$$5x + 8 \leq 10x$$
$$5x + 8 - 5x \leq 10x - 5x$$

$$3(6x - 2) = 12$$
$$18x - 6 = 12$$

Two operations that undo each other, such as addition and subtraction.

Lesson 3 Solve One-Step Multiplication and Division Inequalities with Positive Coefficients

English Learner Instructional Strategy

Vocabulary Support: Build Background Knowledge

Before the lesson, write: *inequality, inequalities*. Underline the base word *equal* in both. Ask, *What does this mean?* **same or equivalent** Then circle the prefix *in-* in both words. Tell students that these letters form the prefix *in-*, which means "not." Finally, circle the letters *ity* in the first word and tell students that the suffix means "state of being." Explain how this suffix makes the word *inequality* a noun, or a word that names a thing. Then help students put together all the word parts to define *inequality* as "something that is not equal."

Compare the spellings of *inequality* and *inequalities*. Point out the plural ending *-es* in *inequalities*. Explain that *-es* shows the word names more than one thing. Therefore, the word *inequalities* means "two or more things that are unequal." Display photos or drawings that illustrate *inequalities,* such as two glasses filled with different amounts of juice or a large set of coins versus a small set. Finally, show the math symbols: $>$, $<$, $\geq$, $\leq$.

Math Language Routine: Three Reads

Ensure comprehension of the Apply problem on page 353 of the Student Book.
1st Read: Make sure students understand that an equal number of each item is purchased, but the costs of the items are different.
2nd Read: Support students in understanding that in order to find how much money will be left, Scarlett needs to find how many items she can purchase.
3rd Read: Brainstorm ways to find how much money she will have left.

English Language Development Leveled Activities

Entering/Emerging	Developing/Expanding	Bridging
Developing Oral Language	**Building Oral Language**	**Logical Reasoning**
Write the inequality $5x < 20$ on the board. Read the statement aloud with students: **Five times *x* is less than twenty.** Then say, *Let's solve the inequality. Should we multiply or divide?* **divide** *What is 5x divided by 5?* **x** *What is 20 divided by 5?* **4** Write: $x < 4$. Ask, *What does this say?* **x is less than four.** Now write the inequality $\frac{x}{7} > 12$ on the board. Read the statement aloud with students: **x divided by 7 is greater than 12.** Follow similar steps to solve this inequality.	Write the following example on the board: *Of the numbers 4, 5, 6, which is a solution of the inequality 2f < 9?* Teach and model cause-and-effect sentences. Students can then describe their reasoning for why a value could be a solution to an inequality or why it could not. Say, *I know that 4 is a possible solution for x because 2 times 4 is less than 9.* Model the sentence again and have students repeat it chorally and then individually. Repeat with this cause-and-effect sentence, *I know that 5 is not a possible solution because 2 times 5 is greater than 9.*	Ask, *How can you check your solution to an inequality?* Have partners work together to determine an answer. Have them first discuss and then write their theories. Then have them use a mathematical example to illustrate it. **We can check a solution to an inequality by _____. We can show this by using the example _____. We can [word backward/substitute a number/and so on] to show that _____ is a possible solution.**

Lesson 3 Notetaking

Solve One-Step Multiplication and Division Inequalities with Positive Coefficients

Use Cornell notes to better understand the lesson's concepts. Complete each sentence by filling in the blanks with the correct word or phrase.

Questions	Notes
1. What are the Multiplication or Division Properties of Inequality	If $a > b$, then $\frac{a}{c} > \frac{b}{c}$ and $\underline{ac} > bc$ (where $c > 0$). If $a < b$, then $\frac{a}{c} < \frac{b}{c}$ and $ac < \underline{bc}$ (where $c > 0$). The same is true for $a \geq b$ or $\underline{a \leq b}$.
2. What do the Multiplication Property of Inequality and the Division Property of Inequality state about positive numbers?	If an inequality has a positive $\underline{coefficient}$, the inequality will stay the same if I divide or multiply $\underline{each\ side}$ of an inequality by the same $\underline{positive}$ number.

Summary

How can I solve the inequality $5x \leq 23$? See students' work.

_____

_____

_____

_____

_____

_____

Lesson 4 Solve One-Step Multiplication and Division Inequalities with Negative Coefficients

English Learner Instructional Strategy

Vocabulary Support: Activate Prior Knowledge

Help students recall what they know about multiplying and dividing positive and negative integers. Write: $5 \cdot 2 = w$; $-3 \cdot 4 = x$; $10 \div (-2) = y$; $-15 \div 5 = z$. Point to the first equation and ask, *Is w a positive or negative number?* **positive** *How do you know?* **Both factors have the same sign.** Point to the second equation and ask, *Is x a positive or negative number?* **negative** *How do you know?* **The factors have different signs.** Point to the third equation and ask, *Is y a positive or negative number?* **negative** *How do you know?* **The dividend is positive. Its divisor and quotient must have the same signs.** Point to the last equation and ask, *Is z a positive or negative number?* **negative** *How do you know?* **The dividend is negative. Its divisor and quotient must have different signs.**

Math Language Routine: Collect and Display

As students discuss how multiplying or dividing each side of an inequality by the same negative number affects the inequality, write key words and phrases you hear, such as *reversed, divided,* and *inequality.* Display the words and phrases for student reference throughout the lesson.

English Language Development Leveled Activities

Entering/Emerging	Developing/Expanding	Bridging
Word Recognition	**Show What You Know**	**Share What You Know**
Write an inequality with a negative coefficient on the board. When teaching students that the inequality symbol must be reversed if multiplying or dividing each side by a negative number, write the word *reverse* on the board. Say, *We reverse the symbol.* Write the sentence and have students repeat. Then introduce other words that can be used in place of *reverse,* such as *change, switch,* or *swap.* For each word, say the new sentence and have students repeat: *We switch the symbol.*	Organize students into pairs. Ask each pair to write two inequality problems, one for multiplication and one for division. Challenge students to have a negative coefficient in one of the inequalities. Then have them exchange problems with another pair of students. Tell partners to work together to solve the problems they received. Then have them present the problems and explain their solutions to the class, using these sentence frames: **[Multiply/Divide] both sides of the inequality by _____. The variable is [less than/greater than] _____.**	Have students work in pairs. Give each pair a set of one-step inequalities to solve, along with these guidelines: *1) One partner reads the first inequality aloud. 2) The other partner states which property of inequality to use to solve the inequality. 3) Reverse roles on the next inequality.* Once they have completed the inequality problems, have them describe when and why they need to change the direction of an inequality symbol.

NAME _____ DATE _____ PERIOD _____

Lesson 4 Review Vocabulary

Solve One-Step Multiplication and Division Inequalities with Negative Coefficients

Use the three-column chart to organize the vocabulary in this lesson.
Write the word in Spanish. Then complete each definition.

English	Spanish	Definition
coefficient	coeficiente	The numerical factor of a term that contains a __variable__
Division Property of Inequality	propiedad de desigualdad en la división	When you divide __each side__ of an inequality by a negative number, the inequality symbol must be __reversed__ for the inequality to remain true.
Multiplication Property of Inequality	propiedad de desigualdad en la multiplicación	When you __multiply__ each side of an inequality by a negative number, the __inequality__ symbol must be __reversed__ for the inequality to remain true.
negative	negativo	A number that is less than __zero__.

Lesson 5 Write and Solve One-Step Multiplication and Division Inequalities

English Learner Instructional Strategy

Collaborative Support: Act It Out

Write the following real-world problem on the board: *Five players on the soccer team scored goals this season. Eddie scored 3 goals, Max scored 13, Yeshi scored 8, and Aiden scored 9.* Then teach or review this vocabulary from the problem: *goal, soccer team, scored, scorers, season.* Define the words using photos and demonstrations. Have groups of students prepare a skit. Have each student in the group take on one of the following roles: Eddie, Max, Yeshi, or Aiden. Have the "scorers" compare their total number of goals, using the sentence frame, I scored [more/fewer] goals than you scored. Review the difference between *less than* and *fewer than; fewer than* is used with things that can be counted (such as *goals* or *points*). Have each scorer compare to all three of the other scorers and then write an inequality, both mathematically and in words, to describe the relationships.

Math Language Routine: Stronger and Clearer Each Time

Have students individually write their response to the Apply problem on Student Book page 369, then pair up with another student to refine and clarify their responses through conversation. Students then revise their initial written response and repeat with a new partner.

English Language Development Leveled Activities

Entering/Emerging	Developing/Expanding	Bridging
Developing Oral Language	**Building Oral Language**	**Share What You Know**
Distribute a number of pennies to each student. Have students count their pennies and then compare numbers with other students. Have them use the sentence frames **I have [more/fewer] pennies than _____. I have as many pennies as _____.**	Repeat the Entering/Emerging activity. After students have mastered the sentence frames with the subject *I*, model and prompt new frames using classmates' names as the subject. For example, **James has [more/fewer] pennies than I do. James has as many pennies as I do.**	Have a Bridging student act as a mentor and help an Entering/Emerging or Developing/Expanding student identify the key words that indicate which inequality symbol to use in each of the problems in the lesson. In the first example in the lesson, for instance, mentors might say, **They key words are *at least* $120. Does that mean greater than $120 or less than $120? Does it include $120 or not?** They should also help the partner make a list of the signal words in their math notebooks.

NAME _____ DATE _____ PERIOD _____

Lesson 5 Vocabulary

Write and Solve One-Step Multiplication and Division Inequalities

Draw a line to connect each example to the phrase that best completes the sentence.

$4x$ is ___$4x < b$___ b.

$18q$ minus 23 is ___$18q - 23 > r$___ r.

less than

$3x$ minus $2y$ is ___$3x - 2y \leq 6z$___ $6z$.

less than or equal to

$\frac{1}{2}m$ is ___$\frac{1}{2}m \geq 2n$___ $2n$.

greater than

$6x$ is ___$6x \leq 13$___ 13.

greater than or equal to

$7a$ plus 14 is ___$7a + 14 > 56b$___ $56b$.

$\frac{4}{7}c$ is ___$\frac{4}{7}c \geq \frac{2}{3}d$___ $\frac{2}{3}d$.

Course 2 · Module 7 *Write and Solve Inequalities*   **39**

Lesson 6 Write and Solve Two-Step Inequalities

English Learner Instructional Strategy

Collaborative Support: Numbered Heads Together

Organize students into groups of four and assign a number 1 to 4 to each student. Have the small groups work together on the following problems: $5x - 7 \geq 43$ and $11 \leq 7 + \frac{x}{5}$. They should discuss each problem, agree on a solution, and ensure that everyone in the group understands and can give the answer. When it is time to review the answer, call out a random number from 1 to 4. The students assigned to that number should raise their hands, and when called on, will answer for the team. Encourage the following language:

Entering/Emerging: **Is this correct? I (don't) understand.**

Developing/Expanding: **Do you get it? I (don't) understand. I can answer this.**
I (don't) agree.

Bridging: **Do you think you can answer this? I can give the answer.**
I'm afraid I don't agree with your answer.

Math Language Routine: Discussion Supports

As students engage in discussing the Talk About It question on Student Book page 377, restate statements they make as a question to seek clarification and to confirm comprehension that the solution of the inequality is not necessarily the answer to the problem. Encourage students to challenge each other's ideas when warranted.

English Language Development Leveled Activities

Entering/Emerging	Developing/Expanding	Bridging
Developing Oral Language	**Partners Work/Pairs Share**	**Share What You Know**
Write the inequalities $3x - 4 \leq 8$, $2x + 5 \geq 15$, $\frac{x}{2} + 5 > 4$, and $\frac{x}{5} - 7 < -3$ on the board. Point to each inequality and say, *This inequality has two* **operations**. Point to the inequality symbol and ask, *What does this mean?* Write these possible responses on the board, and have students point to the correct one: **less than, less than or equal to, greater than, greater than or equal to.** Then ask, *How do I solve the inequality?*	Divide students into pairs. Then write and read aloud this problem: *A tutoring company charges $60 to enroll plus $20 per session. Moira does not want to spend more than $100 for tutoring. How many tutoring sessions can she have?* Direct partners to write and solve an inequality based on this word problem. **$60 + 20x \leq 100$** Then have them interpret the solution, using this sentence frame: **Moira can have _____ tutoring sessions.** Finally, have them check their answer against that of another pair of students.	Direct students to write and solve a two-step inequality of their own. Then have them explain their two-step inequality to an Entering/Emerging or Developing/Expanding peer, guiding their partner through the solution. Permit native language use for clarification. Finally, have the Entering/Emerging or Developing/Expanding student report back to you with the solution.

NAME _____ DATE _____ PERIOD _____

Lesson 6 Vocabulary
Write and Solve Two-Step Inequalities

Use the definition map to list qualities about the vocabulary word or phrase.
Sample answers are given.

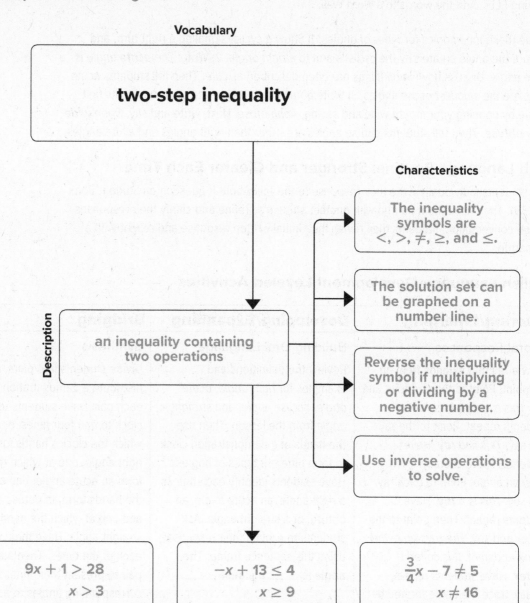

Vocabulary

two-step inequality

Description

an inequality containing
two operations

Characteristics

The inequality
symbols are
$<$, $>$, $\neq$, $\geq$, and $\leq$.

The solution set can
be graphed on a
number line.

Reverse the inequality
symbol if multiplying
or dividing by a
negative number.

Use inverse operations
to solve.

$9x + 1 > 28$
$x > 3$

$-x + 13 \leq 4$
$x \geq 9$

$\frac{3}{4}x - 7 \neq 5$
$x \neq 16$

Write and solve examples.

Lesson 1 Vertical and Adjacent Angles

English Learner Instructional Strategy

Sensory Support: Mnemonics

Write *congruent, adjacent angles, obtuse angle,* and *vertex* and their Spanish cognates, *congruente, ángulos adyacentes, ángulo obtuso,* and *vértice,* respectively. Introduce the words, and provide math examples. Use other translation tools for non-Spanish speaking ELLs. Add the words to a Word Wall.

Provide these mnemonics for types of angles: 1) Show a cyclist signaling a right turn, and compare the angle created by the cyclist's arm to a *right angle.* 2) Write: *The **acute** angle is a cute angle.* Discuss how *small* things are often described as *cute.* Then tell students acute angles are the *smallest* of the angles. 3) Write *obtuse* and exaggerate pronouncing its first syllable by opening your mouth wide and saying, *Ahhh-btuse.* Next, write and say, *Open **wide** to say **obtuse**.* Then tell students obtuse angles are *wider* than right angles and acute angles.

Math Language Routine: Stronger and Clearer Each Time

Have students individually write their response to the Talk About It question on Student Book page 391. Then have them pair up with another student to refine and clarify their responses through conversation. Students then revise their initial written response and repeat with a new partner.

English Language Development Leveled Activities

Entering/Emerging	Developing/Expanding	Bridging
Choral Responses Draw a ray that extends from an endpoint. Point to the endpoint and say, *This is an **endpoint**.* Have students repeat. Point to the ray and say, *This is a **ray**.* Have students repeat chorally. Then draw an angle. Point to each ray and say, *This is a **ray**.* Have students repeat. Then point to the vertex and say, *The rays have the **same** endpoint. It is called a **vertex**.* Have students repeat. Finally, trace the angle formed by the two rays, and say, *This is an **angle**.* Have students repeat. Randomly point to each part of the angle and have students name it chorally.	**Building Oral Language** Review the definitions and examples for *right angle, acute angle, obtuse angle,* and *straight angle* from the lesson. Then use the hands of a demonstration clock to form different types of angles. Have students identify each one as a right angle, an acute angle, an obtuse, or a straight angle. Ask students to explain their responses using this sentence frame: **The angle is _____ because _____.**	**Synthesis** Divide students into pairs, and distribute a demonstration clock to each pair. Have students use the clock to find four times: one at which the clock's hands form a right angle, one at which the hands form an acute angle, one at which the hands form an obtuse angle, and one at which the hands form a straight angle. Have them write each of the times. Then ask each pair to present their times and corresponding angles to an Entering/Emerging student.

NAME _____ DATE _____ PERIOD _____

Lesson 1 Vocabulary
Vertical and Adjacent Angles

Use the three-column chart to write the vocabulary word and
definition for each drawing. Sample answers are given.

What I See	Vocabulary Word	Definition
	vertex	the common endpoint of the rays forming the angle
	right angle	an angle that measures exactly 90°
	acute angle	an angle with a measure greater than 0° and less than 90°
	obtuse angle	any angle that measures greater than 90 but less than 180°
	straight angle	an angle that measures exactly 180°
	vertical angles	opposite angles formed by the intersection of two lines
	congruent angles	angles that have the same measure
	adjacent angles	angles that have the same vertex, share a common side, and do not overlap

Course 2 • Module 8 *Geometric Figures* **41**

Lesson 2 Complementary and Supplementary Angles

English Learner Instructional Strategy

Vocabulary Support: Cognates

Before the lesson, write *complementary angle* and *supplementary angle* and their Spanish cognates, *ángulos complementarios* and *ángulos suplementarios,* respectively, on a Word Wall. Introduce the words, and provide math examples. Utilize other translation tools for non-Spanish speaking ELLs. Discuss multiple meanings for *complementary* and *supplementary*, using pictures/demonstrations to support understanding. Finally, share this mnemonic for supplementary angles. Circle *supple* in *supplementary.* Explain how things described as *supple* are *flexible.* As an example, show a photo of a gymnast performing a split. Then show that the adjacent angles formed by his or her legs and torso are supplementary angles. (Note: The words *supple* and *supplementary* are not related in meaning.)

Math Language Routine: Compare and Connect

Pair students and give them a set of four pairs of angle measures; for example, three pairs of angles are complementary and one is not or three pairs are supplementary and one is not. Students work together to decide which angle pair doesn't belong with the other three. Both students should be prepared to explain their thinking to a different group.

English Language Development Leveled Activities

Entering/Emerging	Developing/Expanding	Bridging
Word Knowledge	**Developing Oral Language**	**Partner Work**
Ensure students understand, that in this lesson, *adjacent* means "connected" rather than "near." Then point out examples. Say, *Our classroom is* **adjacent to** *[Teacher name]'s classroom. Our classrooms are* **adjacent**. *The classrooms share a common wall.* Next, draw several sets of angles, some adjacent and some not. Include complementary and supplementary angles among the adjacent angles. Then ask students to identify the angles in each set as **adjacent** or **not adjacent**. Finally, have them identify adjacent angles as **complementary** or **supplementary.**	Have students work with a partner to identify complementary and supplementary angles. Give pairs samples of adjacent angles, some that are complementary, some that are supplementary, and some that are neither. Ask one student to identify the angles as **complementary**, **supplementary**, or **neither** by sight, and have the other measure the angles and add their measurements to see if they equal 90° or 180°. Tell students to discuss what makes two angles complementary or supplementary.	Have each student create his or her own figure using intersecting lines. Tell students that their figure should include at least one pair of supplementary angles, one pair of complementary angles, and one pair of vertical angles. Have them label all the angles in their figure with a letter, and then exchange papers with a partner. Students should identify complementary, supplementary, and vertical angles in the figure they receive. Then have them check answers with the student who drew the figure.

NAME _____ DATE _____ PERIOD _____

Lesson 2 Vocabulary
Complementary and Supplementary Angles

Use the word cards to define each vocabulary word or phrase and give an example. Sample answers are given.

Word Cards

complementary angles

Definition

Two angles are complementary if the sum of their measures is 90°.

Example Sentence

Angle 1 and angle 2 add up to 90°. They are complementary angles.

ángulos complementarios

Definición

Dos ángulos son complementarios si la suma de sus medidas es 90°.

Word Cards

supplementary angles

Definition

Two angles are supplementary if the sum of their measures is 180°.

Example Sentence

Angle 1 and angle 2 add up to 180°. They are supplementary angles.

ángulos suplementarios

Definición

Dos ángulos son suplementarios si la suma de sus medidas es 180°.

Lesson 3 Triangles
English Learner Instructional Strategy

Language Structure Support: Choral Responses

Write *acute triangle, equilateral triangle, isosceles triangle, scalene triangle,* and *congruent segments,* and their Spanish cognates, *triángulo acutángulo, triángulo equilátero, triángulo isosceles, triángulo escaleno,* and *segmentos congruentes,* respectively. Introduce the words, and provide math examples. Utilize other translation tools for non-Spanish speaking ELLs. Add the words to a Word Wall.

After the lesson, revisit types of triangles by drawing an example of each on the board. Include a right triangle and an obtuse triangle, in addition to those already named in this activity. Then point to each triangle and ask, for example, *Is this an **isosceles** triangle or an **obtuse** triangle?* Have students chorally say the name of the triangle.

Math Language Routine: Co-Craft Questions and Problems

Pair students and have them co-create a problem similar to the Check problem on Student Book page 417. Have them work together to solve their problem and then trade their problem with another pair. After each pair solves the other pair's problems, have them form a group of four to check solutions and correct any mistakes that may have been made. Revisit this routine throughout the lesson for reinforcement.

English Language Development Leveled Activities

Entering/Emerging	Developing/Expanding	Bridging
Word Recognition	**Word Identification**	**Anchor Chart**
Give students pictures of objects or scenes that have triangles in them. The pictures may be printed, photocopied, or torn from a newspaper or magazine. Tell students to trace the outline of each triangle they find in a picture. Then have them label each triangle, using one or more of these names, as appropriate: *acute triangle, obtuse triangle, right triangle, scalene triangle, isosceles triangle,* or *equilateral triangle.* Show students that all triangles can be labeled correctly with more than one name. Have students show their labeled pictures to the class.	Have students make flashcards for the different types of triangles described in this lesson. On one side of the card, tell them to write the term. On the other side, have them write a definition and then draw and label an example. Encourage students to include terms/cognates from their native language to help describe the triangles on the flashcards. When cards are completed, have students work in pairs to quiz each other using the flashcards. Encourage students to create a pocket in their math notebook to store the cards for future reference.	Tell students that many triangles have common features. Have partners work together to answer these questions about the triangles from this lesson: *Which triangles always have all acute angles?* **acute triangle, equilateral triangle** *Which triangles have no congruent sides?* **scalene triangles** *Which triangles always have at least two congruent sides?* **isosceles triangle, equilateral triangle** *After partners have answered the questions, ask them to make a chart that summarizes their findings.*

NAME _____ DATE _____ PERIOD _____

Lesson 3 Vocabulary

Triangles

Use the three-column chart to write the vocabulary word and definition for each drawing. Sample answers are given.

What I See	Vocabulary Word	Definition
Name by **angles**	acute triangle	a triangle with three acute angles
	right triangle	a triangle with one right angle
	obtuse triangle	a triangle with one obtuse angle
Name by **sides**	scalene triangle	a triangle with no congruent sides
	isosceles triangle	a triangle with at least two congruent sides
	equilateral triangle	a triangle with three congruent sides
General vocabulary	triangle	a figure with three sides and three angles
	congruent segments	sides that are the same length

Course 2 · Module 8 *Geometric Figures* **43**

Lesson 4 · Scale Drawings

English Learner Instructional Strategy

Sensory Support: Illustrations, Diagrams, and Drawings

Before the lesson, write *scale model* and *scale factor* and their Spanish cognates, *modelo a escala* and *factor de escala,* respectively. Introduce the words, and provide math examples to support understanding. Utilize other appropriate translation tools for non-Spanish speaking ELLs. Add the words to a Word Wall.

During the lesson, show students an assortment of maps, and point out the scale on each. Use the scales to estimate the number of miles or kilometers between cities, states, and countries. Also, show students other examples of scale models and drawings, such as floor plan samples from home improvement magazines, architect's blue prints, and needlework guides.

Math Language Routine: Critique, Correct, and Clarify

Make a false claim for students to critique; for example, *In order to be proportional, measurements in a scale drawing must be in the same unit of measurement as the original. Am I correct?* Ask students to correct the statement, explaining how they know it is incorrect. Revisit this routine throughout the lesson to provide reinforcement.

English Language Development Leveled Activities

Entering/Emerging	Developing/Expanding	Bridging
Listen and Write	**Look, Listen, and Identify**	**Partner Work**
Show and explain what a statue is and who Thomas Jefferson was. Then write this problem: *Thomas Jefferson was x feet tall. A statue of him is 19 feet tall. The scale for the statue is 3 feet = 1 foot. What is the value of x?* Write and say the reworded problem. Then have partners work together to write and solve an expression to find Thomas Jefferson's height.	Write and say the following word problem: *Ted is making a scale drawing of a kitchen. The kitchen measures 9 feet by 12 feet. The scale for the drawing is 1 inch equals 3 feet.* Have students use the scale to draw the kitchen on 1-inch grid paper. Then have them answer these questions: *What are the actual dimensions of the scale drawing?* **3 inches by 4 inches** *Will the scale drawing by larger or smaller than the actual kitchen?* **smaller**	Have partners measure the dimensions of the classroom and round the measurements to the nearest foot. Then have students make a scale drawing of the room. Tell them to choose a scale, keeping in mind that their drawings will need to fit on a piece of grid paper. Then have them make their drawings. Each student should work individually and then compare papers with his or her partner. Have partners note how their drawings are alike and different. Discuss as a class why the sizes of drawings may differ but their shapes should not.

Lesson 4 Vocabulary
Scale Drawings

Use the vocabulary squares to write a definition, a sentence, and an example for each vocabulary word. **Sample answers are given.**

scale drawing	Definition
	a drawing that is used to represent objects that are too large or too small to be drawn at actual size

Example	Sentence
	A scale drawing was used to show the furniture placement in the room.

scale model	Definition
	a model used to represent objects that are too large or too small to be built at actual size

Example	Sentence
	A scale model was used to represent the 15 story building.

scale factor	Definition
	a scale written as ratio without units in simplest form

Example	Sentence
$\frac{1}{18}$	The scale of a model is 1 in = 1.5 feet. The scale factor is $\frac{1}{18}$.

44   **Course 2 · Module 8** *Geometric Figures*

Lesson 5 Three-Dimensional Figures

English Learner Instructional Strategy

Vocabulary Support: Cognates

Before the lesson, write *prism, base, pyramid, plane, coplanar, cylinder,* and *cone,* and their Spanish cognates, *prisma, base, pirámide, plano, coplanar, cilindro,* and *cono,* respectively. Introduce the words, and provide math examples. Utilize other translation tools for non-Spanish speaking ELLs. Add the words to a Word Wall.

Discuss multiple meanings for these words: *prism, base, plane, cone.* Use real-world objects, photos, and demonstrations to support understanding. Finally, tell students that these words are homophones: *base/bass, plane/plain.* Discuss multiple meanings for *bass* and *plain.*

Math Language Routine: Collect and Display

As students describe the three-dimensional figures, write key words and phrases you hear, such as *horizontal, vertical, plane,* and *cross-section.* Display the words and phrases for student reference throughout the lesson. Update the collection with other relevant terms and new understandings as the lesson progresses.

English Language Development Leveled Activities

Entering/Emerging	Developing/Expanding	Bridging
Anchor Chart	**Word Identification**	**Word Knowledge**
Draw and label the vertices of a large rectangular prism and a large triangular prism. Ask volunteers to come to the board and identify an edge, a face, a base, and a vertex on each prism. If students are having difficulty, help them start an anchor chart for three-dimensional figures that includes the name of each figure and a diagram showing what the figure looks like with its parts labeled.	Have students make flashcards for the vocabulary words in this lesson. Write and discuss these guidelines: *1) On one side of the card, write the term. 2) On the other side of the card, write a definition. Include a drawing.* Encourage students to use words/cognates from their native language to help define and describe the terms on the flashcards. After they have had time to work, have partners quiz each using their flashcards.	Have partners make a list of vocabulary words and other terms introduced in this lesson. Then have them use a dictionary to determine which terms have multiple meanings. Remind students that some vocabulary words with multiple meanings were discussed before the lesson. Others that students should address include *face, edge,* and *vertex.* Have students discuss how the meanings for each word differ and whether or not the various meanings seem to be related at all. Have students make a table to organize their findings. Then invite them to present their tables to the class.

NAME _____ DATE _____ PERIOD _____

Lesson 5 Vocabulary
Three-Dimensional Figures

Use the three-column chart to organize the vocabulary in this lesson. Write the
word in Spanish. Then write the definition of each word. Sample answers are given.

English	Spanish	Definition
polyhedron	poliedro	three-dimensional figure, or solid, with flat surfaces that are polygons
prism	prisma	a 3D figure with at least three rectangular lateral faces and top and bottom faces are parallel
base	base	In a prism, the pair of parallel, congruent faces. In a pyramid, the polygon containing the base edge of the, lateral, triangular faces.
pyramid	pirámide	a 3D figure with at least three lateral faces that are triangles and only one base
face	cara	a flat surface of a polyhedron
edge	borde	the line segment where two faces of the polyhedron intersect
vertex	vértice	the point where three or more planes intersect
cylinder	cilindro	a 3D figure with two parallel congruent circular bases connected by a curved surface
cone	cono	a 3D figure one circular base connected by a curved side to a single point

Lesson 1 Circumference of Circles
English Learner Instructional Strategy

Vocabulary Support: Word Knowledge

Before the lesson, write *radius, center,* and *pi* and their Spanish cognates, *radio, centro,* and *pi,* respectively. Introduce the words, and provide math examples. Utilize other translation tools for non-Spanish speaking ELLs. Then discuss these word features: 1) *Radius* contains the root word *rad,* meaning "ray." Help students relate the meaning of *ray* to the meaning of *radius.* 2) Pronounce *center,* emphasizing the /s/ at the beginning of the word. Then give students this tip for remembering the pronunciation: *c* followed by *e* or *i* usually makes this sound in English: /s/. Invite other examples of words with /s/ spelled *ce* or *ci.* **Sample response:** <u>c</u>ircumferen<u>ce</u> 3) Pronounce *pi* and then tell students that this word is a homophone of *pie.* Use a photo or illustration to help you define *pie.*

Add the words and their cognates to a Word Wall along with math examples.

Math Language Routine: Co-Craft Questions and Problems

Pair students and have them co-create a problem similar to the Check problem on Student Book page 450. Have them work together to solve their problem and then trade their problem with another pair. After each pair solves the other pair's problems, have them form a group of four to check solutions and correct any mistakes that may have been made. Revisit this routine throughout the lesson for reinforcement.

English Language Development Leveled Activities

Entering/Emerging	Developing/Expanding	Bridging
Anchor Chart	**Number Game**	**Share What You Know**
Distribute these materials to groups of students: scissors, glue, construction paper, poster board, string, an adhesive dot, drinking straws. Have each group cut a different sized circle from the construction paper and then mount it on poster board. Next have students attach the following to their circles: a center point made with the dot, a radius and a diameter cut from straws, and a circumference made of string. Have groups label each part of their completed model with the correct vocabulary term and definition. Compile students' work onto an anchor chart and post for students to use as a reference.	Give partners a number cube, a compass, a ruler, and a piece of string. Then discuss these game rules: *1) One student rolls the number cube. The number rolled is a circle's radius in inches. Use the compass to draw a circle with that radius. 2) The other student uses the string and ruler to measure the circle's circumference. Then he or she uses the formula C = πd to find the circumference of the circle. Record both circumference measurements and compare them. Are they similar? 3) Partners switch roles to play the next round.* Have students play a few rounds.	Divide students into pairs and tell them they will be working together on a research project about how different cultures use circles in art. Share examples of circle art, such as "eternity" bands and Native American dream catchers. Then ask pairs to choose a type of circle art to research. If students need ideas, you might suggest the Olympic rings, flag art, mandalas, or even the "circle of life" diagrams found in science textbooks. Have pairs create a poster showing examples of their chosen art, notes about its meaning, and the history of its use. Then ask them to share their posters with the class.

NAME _____ DATE _____ PERIOD _____

Lesson 1 Vocabulary
Circumference of Circles

Use the three column chart to write the vocabulary word and definition for each drawing. Sample answers are given.

What I See	Vocabulary Word	Definition
(circle)	circle	the set of all points in a plane that are the same distance from a given point called the center
(circle with center point)	center	the point from which all points on circle are the same distance
(circle with dashed outline)	circumference	the distance around a circle
(circle with diameter line)	diameter	the distance across a circle through its center
(circle with radius line)	radius	the distance from the center of a circle to any point on the circle
π	pi	the ratio of the circumference of a circle to its diameter

Lesson 2 Area of Circles

English Learner Instructional Strategy

Sensory Support: Mnemonics

Before the lesson, write *semicircle* and its Spanish cognate, *semicirculo*. Introduce the word, and show an example. Utilize other translation tools for non-Spanish speaking ELLs. Then underline *semi* and tell students these letters form a prefix that means "half." Help students use the meaning of *semi-* to define *semicircle* as "a half circle." Then show students how two semicircles put together form a full circle.

Draw the sign ($\approx$) for "approximately equals." Help students remember its meaning by showing its likeness to the equals sign and to ocean waves. Discuss how, like waves show a surface isn't perfectly flat, the "approximately equals" sign shows an equation isn't perfectly precise.

Math Language Routine: Compare and Connect

Think aloud about the question *How can you use the formula for the area of a parallelogram to help you find the area of a circle?* using comparative terms such as *both* to model the language of expressing how two things are related. Encourage input from students regarding how the wavy parallelogram relates to the number of sectors.

English Language Development Leveled Activities

Entering/Emerging	Developing/Expanding	Bridging
Word Knowledge	**Share What You Know**	**Show What You Know**
Differentiate math meanings for *square*. Say, *A square is a* **figure**. Show students pictures of geometric figures, identifying each. Then say, *A square is a* **measurement**. Use a ruler to draw a 3-inch line. Say, *This measurement is 3 inches*. Then draw a rectangle that is 3 inches in width and 1 inch in height. Say, *This measurement is 3* **square** *inches*. Finally, say, *I can* **square** *a number*. Write and discuss: the **square** of 3; 3 **squared** $= 3 \times 3$ or 3^2.	Give each student a different-sized circle. Circles may be drawn and cut out, or they may be classroom objects. Ask students to write step-by-step instructions for applying the formula for area to their circles. Have them use this guide: **Start with this formula: _____. Then, measure the circle's _____. My circle's _____ measures _____ [units]. Use the measurement in place of this part of the formula: _____. Then, multiply. The area of my circle is _____ square [units].**	Ask, *What are two formulas for finding the circumference of a circle?* Invite volunteers to come to the board and write one of the formulas. $A = 3.14r^2$, $A = \frac{22}{7}r^2$ Then point to the one that uses a fraction. Ask, *When and why should we use this formula?* Have students write their explanations in their notebooks. Then invite volunteers to share their explanations with the class.

Multicultural Teacher Tip

Mathematical notation varies from culture to culture, so you may find ELLs using unfamiliar symbols in place of standard U.S. symbols. For example, students from Latin American countries may use a point in place of $\times$ to show multiplication. Although the point is also commonly used in the US, the placement and size may vary depending on the native culture. In Mexico, the point is larger and set higher between the numbers than in the U.S. In some Latin American countries, the point is set low and can be confused with a decimal point.

NAME _____ DATE _____ PERIOD _____

Lesson 2 Vocabulary
Area of Circles

Use the definition map to list qualities about the vocabulary word or phrase.
Sample answers are given.

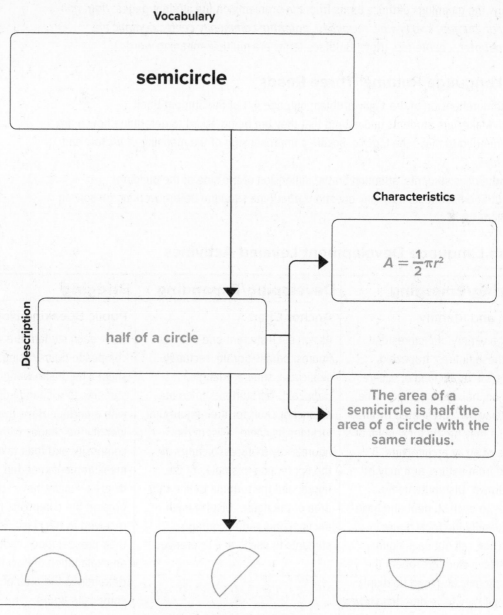

Vocabulary

semicircle

Characteristics

$$A = \frac{1}{2}\pi r^2$$

Description

half of a circle

The area of a semicircle is half the area of a circle with the same radius.

Draw examples of semicircles.

Course 2 · Module 9 *Measure Figures* **47**

Lesson 3 Area of Composite Figures
English Learner Instructional Strategy

Sensory Support: Realia, Photographs, and Physical Activities

Write *composite figure* and its Spanish cognate, *figura compuesto* on the Word Wall. Introduce the term, and provide a math example. Utilize other translation tools for non-Spanish speaking ELLs.

Then show the meanings of these terms from the problems on the student pages: *flag*, *non-rectangular, burgee, swallowtail, reclaimed, painting; community center, ceramic tile, mosaic, counter, countertop*. (Note: Boldface terms are multiple-meaning words.)

Math Language Routine: Three Reads

Ensure comprehension of the Apply problem on page 471 of the Student Book.
1st Read: Make sure students understand that they are being asked to determine how many tiles are needed to make the mosaic. Ensure comprehension of the meaning of *mosaic* and *ceramic tiles*.
2nd Read: Focus students' attention on the dimension of the side of the building.
3rd Read: See if students have any questions about the situation before working on solving the problem.

English Language Development Leveled Activities

Entering/Emerging	Developing/Expanding	Bridging
Listen and Identify	**Anchor Chart**	**Public Speaking Norms**
Collect a variety of pictures that show these figures: trapezoid, triangle, circle, rectangle, square, pentagon, hexagon, octagon. The figure may be represented by an object, it may be the focal point of a piece of art or architecture, it may be from nature, or it may be hand drawn. Distribute a few pictures to each student and have them identify the focal figure in each. Then call out each figure name. Have students repeat the name chorally and then hold up a picture, if they have one that shows the figure. Encourage students to identify features that help them classify the figure.	Assign each student one of these figures: parallelogram, rectangle, semicircle, square, triangle, trapezoid. Tell students to create an anchor chart for their figure that includes its name, a list of the figure's key features, pictures of the figure, non-examples of the figure, and the formula to find the area of the figure. Display each anchor chart and encourage students to use it as a reference.	Have each student draw a composite figure, using whatever shapes he or she wants. Then ask students to exchange drawings with a partner. Have the partner identify the shapes within the composite and then take the measurements needed to calculate its area. Finally, have students present the composite figures they received to the class. Tell them their presentations should include an explanation of how they determined the area of the composite figure.

NAME _____ DATE _____ PERIOD _____

Lesson 3 Notetaking
Area of Composite Figures

Use Cornell notes to better understand the lesson's concepts. Complete each
sentence by filling in the blanks with the correct word or phrase.

Questions	Notes
1. How do I find the area of a composite figure?	Since a composite figure is made up of two or more _____shapes_____ , decompose the composite figure. Decompose it into shapes with known _____area_____ formulas. Then find the _____sum_____ of these _____areas_____ .
2. How do I find the area of a shaded region?	Use shapes with _____area formulas_____ that are known. For example, find the area of a region larger than the shaded region and _____subtract_____ the non-shaded regions.

Summary
How do measurements help you describe real-world objects? See students' work.

_____

_____

_____

_____

_____

_____

_____

Lesson 4 Volume
English Learner Instructional Strategy

Collaborative Support: Numbered Heads Together

Organize students into four groups. Give each student in the group a number from one to four. Have groups work together to solve the problems in the lesson. For each problem, tell them to agree on a solution and ensure everyone in their group understands and can give an answer. Work through the problems with students. For each item, call out a number (1–4) randomly. The students assigned to that number should raise their hands and, when called on, answer for their team.

Math Language Routine: Information Gap

Have pairs of students play *Find the Dimension*. Give Student *A* a card with the volume of a pyramid. Give Student *B* a different card with either the area of the base or the height. Student *A* asks Student *B* for the dimension and then determines the missing dimension. Students then switch roles. Encourage students clarify their findings through conversation.

English Language Development Leveled Activities

Entering/Emerging	Developing/Expanding	Bridging
Phonemic Awareness	**Word Knowledge**	**Public Speaking Norms**
Write *face* on the board and pronounce it with students. Take care in enunciating the initial /f/, a sound that does not transfer from all languages. If students need help, show them they can make the sound by biting their lower lip and blowing lightly. Then discuss meanings for *face*. Show students that, within the context of this lesson, a *face* is a side of an object that is on the *outside* of the object. Demonstrate using a paper box. Point to different sides of the box saying, *This is a* **face**. *It is on the* **outside**. Then point to its inside surfaces saying, *This is* **not** *a face. It is on the* **inside**.	Write *face* on the board and pronounce it with students. Remind them that *c* followed by *e* makes this sound: /s/. Then show students that, within the context of this lesson, a *face* is a side on the *outside* of the object. Demonstrate this meaning as shown in the Entering/Emerging Level activity. Then write and say *lateral*. Explain and show that something described as *lateral* appears on the *side* of an object, as opposed to its top or bottom. Now, show students two photos, one of a climber at the top of a mountain and one of a climber scaling a cliff. Ask, *Which climber is on a lateral face?* **the climber on the cliff**	Have students write real-world problems of their own. Then have students exchange papers with a partner. Have the partner solve the problem he or she received and then share the problem and solution with the class.

NAME _____ DATE _____ PERIOD _____

Lesson 4 Vocabulary

Volume

Use the flow chart to review the processes for finding the volume of a prism or pyramid. Sample answers are given.

Volume
Define volume.

the number of cubic units needed to fill

the space occupied by a solid

Determine the type of three-dimensional object.

Prism
Define prism.

a polyhedron with two

parallel and congruent

faces called bases

Pyramid
Define pyramid.

A polyhedron with a base that

is a polygon and three or more

triangular faces that meet in a

common vertex

Write the formula to find the volume of a prism.

$V = Bh$

Write the formula to find the volume of a pyramid.

$V = \frac{1}{3} Bh$

Lesson 5 Surface Area

English Learner Instructional Strategy

Vocabulary Support: Make Connections

Before the lesson, write *surface area* and its Spanish cognate, *área de superficie* on the Word Wall. Introduce the term, and provide a math example. Utilize other translation tools for non-Spanish speaking ELLs. Then discuss multiple meanings for *surface.* Help students understand that, within the context of this lesson, *surface* is an adjective. However, *surface* also has noun and verb meanings. For example, noun meanings of *surface* include "the outside layer of something" and "information that has become public," and verb meanings include "to appear or become visible" and "to cover a surface with a coat of something, such as asphalt." Discuss with students how all these meanings for surface are related. Guide students to understand that all have to do with the *outside* of something, or the part of something that people can easily see or know.

Math Language Routine: Discussion Supports

As students engage in discussing the Talk About It question on Student Book page 488, restate statements they make as a question to seek clarification and to confirm comprehension that the structure of the prism leads to the formula. Encourage students to challenge each other's ideas when warranted.

English Language Development Leveled Activities

Entering/Emerging	Developing/Expanding	Bridging
Read and Write	**Sentence Frames**	**Number Game**
Write the following problem on the board: *Make a rectangular prism. The dimensions must be whole numbers. The maximum surface area is 160 square feet. Maximize the volume in your prism.* Ask, *What kind of prism is it? Is it* **rectangular** *or* **triangular**? **rectangular** Then say, *Here are the rules. 1) Use whole numbers. 2) Use the greatest volume possible. 3) Use the least surface area possible. 4) The maximum surface area is 160 square feet.* Show the meanings of *greatest, least,* and *maximum.* Then work through the problem with students.	Write the following dimensions: length = 9 inches, width = 6 inches, and height = 3 inches. Then say, *These are the dimensions for a rectangular prism.* Have students draw a model of the prism and label its length, width, and height. Then have them write step-by-step instructions for calculating its surface area. Provide these sentence frames for students to use: **This formula shows the area of the prism's top and bottom: ____. This formula shows the area of the prism's front and back: ____. This formula shows the area of the prism's other two sides: ____. The sum of the areas is ____ square inches.**	Organize students into pairs, and give each pair a number cube. Then discuss these game rules: *1) One student rolls the number cube 3 times. The numbers rolled are the dimensions for a rectangular prism. The first number is its length, the second number is its width, and the third number is its height. The student draws the prism and calculates its surface area. 2) The other student takes a turn, repeating the steps in Rule 1. 3) Partners compare surface areas. The student with the greater surface area scores one point. 4) Partners continue taking turns until one student has five points.*

NAME _____ DATE _____ PERIOD _____

Lesson 5 Vocabulary
Surface Area

Use the vocabulary squares to write a definition and a sentence for each
vocabulary word. Sample answers are given.

	Definition
surface area of a prism	the sum of the areas of all of the faces of a prism
Write the formula for a rectangular prism. S.A. = $2\ell h + 2\ell w + 2hw$	Draw a Figure 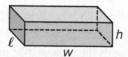

	Definition
slant height of a pyramid	the height of each lateral face
Draw an arrow showing the slant height. 	Sentence The slant height is used to find the surface area of a lateral face of a pyramid.

	Definition
surface area of a pyramid	the sum of all of the faces of a pyramid
Write the formula for a square pyramid. S.A. = $s^2 + 4\left(\dfrac{1}{2}bh\right)$	Draw a Figure 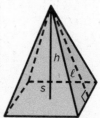

Lesson 6 Volume and Surface Area of Composite Figures

English Learner Instructional Strategy

Collaborative Support: Graffiti Poster

Ask students: *How can you find the* **surface area** *of a three-dimensional composite figure? How can you find its* **volume**? Have students create a graffiti poster and list their ideas about the answers to the questions. Have them include drawings and figures as well. Then have students turn and talk to a neighbor about their ideas. After students have had time to discuss, ask them to share with the class. As students share, make notes on the graffiti poster. Then tell students they will continue working with three-dimensional composite figures in this lesson.

Math Language Routine: Stronger and Clearer Each Time

Have students individually write their responses to the Pause and Reflect questions on Student Book page 497, then pair up with another student to refine and clarify their responses through conversation Students then revise their initial written responses and repeat with a new partner.

English Language Development Leveled Activity

Entering/Emerging	Developing/Expanding	Bridging
Look, Listen, and Identify Present models of several different composite figures to students. Point to each face on a figure and ask, *Does this face have one shape or two shapes?* Have students hold up an index finger if the face has one simple shape, and have them hold up two fingers if the face was made with two simple shapes (such as a triangle on top of a square). Then have students name the shape(s) of each face.	**Think-Pair-Share** Present models of several different composite figures to students. Have students identify the faces of each figure and then tell you the formula they would use to find the area of each face. To extend the activity, have students measure the faces of the figure. Then have them discuss each step for calculating its total surface area with a partner. Finally, ask students to "coach" you through finding the total surface area.	**Cooperative Learning** Divide students into three groups, and assign each group a problem involving three-dimensional composite figures. Have the students in each group work together to: 1) identify the figures used to form each composite figure; 2) decide how to calculate each figure's volume or surface area; and then 3) solve the problem. Once groups have completed their work, have each group present their problem to the other groups. Ask audience members to check the presenting group's calculations and make sure they agree the calculations are correct.

NAME _____ DATE _____ PERIOD _____

Lesson 6 Notetaking

Volume and Surface Area of Composite Figures

Use Cornell notes to better understand the lesson's concepts. Complete each sentence by filling in the blanks with the correct word or phrase.

Questions	Notes
1. How do I find the volume of a composite figure?	Since a composite figure is made up of two or more _____ **three-dimensional figures** _____ , decompose the composite figure. Separate it into solids whose _____ **volume** _____ formulas are known. Then find the _____ **sum** _____ of these _____ **volumes** _____ .
2. How do I find the surface area of a composite figure?	Find the _____ **areas** _____ of the _____ **faces** _____ that make up the composite figure.

Summary
How did the lessons in this chapter help you find the surface area and volume of a composite figure? **See students' work.**
_____
_____
_____
_____
_____
_____

Course 2 · Module 9 *Measure Figures* **51**

Lesson 1 Find Likelihoods

English Learner Instructional Strategy

Vocabulary Support: Communication Guides

Write the following on the board: *certain, impossible, likely, unlikely,* and *equally likely.* Introduce or review each word, and ask students to provide examples of each, if possible. Prompt them with questions such as *What event is certain?* Assist with ideas as necessary.

Write a variety of events on the board, such as: *The sun will (not) rise tomorrow. I will play basketball this afternoon. You can roll a 27 on a number cube. A dog will chase a cat. A cat will chase a dog. One plus one equals three. A coin will land on heads or tails.*

Have students use this sentence frame to report about each scenario: **It is [certain/ impossible/likely/equally likely/unlikely] that ____.**

Math Language Routine: Collect and Display

Create a chart of the table on page 511 of the Student Book and ask students to discuss real-world examples of each kind of event. Write bullet points for each situation under the corresponding words in the table. For example, write *Snows in July in Florida* under *unlikely* on the chart. Display the chart for student reference throughout the lesson. Update the chart with other relevant examples for each word as the lesson progresses.

English Language Development Leveled Activities

Entering/Emerging	Developing/Expanding	Bridging
Basic Vocabulary	**Listen and Identify**	**Build Oral Language**
Write *unlikely* on the board. Review the meaning of *likely* ("a good chance something will happen"). Then underline *un-*. Ask, *What does this word part mean?* **not** Have students give other examples. If they need help, offer *unhappy* or *unknown.* **Note:** The prefix *un-* can also mean "to do the opposite of," as in *untie* or *undo.*	Say a scenario, such as, *When I flip a coin, it will be heads or tails.* Students should use one of the following words to describe the probability: *certain, impossible, likely, unlikely,* and *equally likely.* The first student who correctly answers **certain** gets to come up with the next scenario. Monitor and offer feedback as necessary.	Repeat the Developing/Expanding activity with the following adjustment: instead of making a statement about a scenario, have students formulate a question. Some questions could be fairly complicated, so offer constructive feedback as necessary. Examples include, **What is the likelihood that ____? Is it [certain/ impossible/likely...] that ____? Do you think that ____?**

NAME _____ DATE _____ PERIOD _____

Lesson 1 Vocabulary
Find Likelihoods

Use the vocabulary squares to write a definition, a sentence, and an example for each vocabulary word. Sample answers are given.

likelihood	**Definition** the possibility that something will happen
Example The likelihood of rolling a 1 on a number cube is unlikely	**Sentence** The likelihood that the sun will rise tomorrow is certain.

outcome	**Definition** any one of the possible results of an action
Example 4 is an outcome when a number cube is rolled.	**Sentence** When a number cube is rolled, there are 6 possible outcomes.

event	**Definition** the desired outcome or set of outcomes
Example Rolling a 7 on a single number cube is an impossible event.	**Sentence** In the event that Kevin rolls a 2, he will lose the game.

Lesson 2 Relative Frequency of Simple Events

English Learner Instructional Strategy

Vocabulary Support: Multiple-Meaning Words

Before the lesson, write *relative frequency* and its Spanish cognate, *frecuencia relativa*. Introduce the words, and provide math examples. Utilize other translation tools for non-Spanish speaking ELLs. Post the words on the Word Wall. Next, discuss multiple meanings for both *relative* and *frequency*. Help students remember how these words are used in a statistics context by showing and explaining that the *frequency* of an event is how *often* the event happens. Then write: *relate, relative*. Tell students that *relate* is the base word of *relative*. Show and explain how two things that are *relative* to each other *relate*, or *connect*, to each other somehow. Finally, guide students to see how *relative frequency* shows a relationship between how often an event happens in a certain number of attempts.

Math Language Routine: Co-Craft Questions and Problems

Pair students and have them co-create a problem similar to the Check problem at the bottom of Student Book page 517. Have them work together to solve their problem and then trade their problem with another pair. After each pair solves the other pair's problems, have them form a group of four to check solutions and correct any mistakes that may have been made.

English Language Development Leveled Activities

Entering/Emerging	Developing/Expanding	Bridging
Number Sense	**Act It Out**	**Share What You Know**
Roll a number cube. Show and write the number. Ask, *What are the possible numbers I can roll?* **1, 2, 3, 4, 5, 6** Next, discuss the probability of rolling each number, given 6 chances to roll. Guide students to tell you the probability is $\frac{1}{6}$. Then ask, *What is the probability of rolling a 3 or a 6?* Guide students to tell you the probability of rolling one of these two numbers is $\frac{2}{6}$. Now, write and say: *You will roll the number cube 600 times. The* **probability** *of rolling a 3 or a 6 is $\frac{2}{6}$. How many rolls will be a 3 or a 6?* Have students respond by solving this proportion: $\frac{2 \ rolls}{6 \ rolls} = \frac{x \ rolls}{600 \ rolls}$. **200 rolls** Repeat to find the probability of rolling a 2, 4 or 6.	Repeat the Entering/Emerging activity. Then have each student roll a number cube six times and record each number. Share results as a class. Report results using this sentence frame: **[Student Name] rolls a 3 or 6 ____ times out of 6 rolls.** Then record the class's results using this sentence frame: **The class rolls ____ times out of [number of students times 6] rolls.** Discuss whether the class results show that the relative frequency of rolling a 3 or 6 gets closer to $\frac{2}{6}$ as the number of rolls increases. Repeat the activity to find out what happens as more rolls are added.	Have partners write a relative frequency scenario. After you check the scenario to ensure it makes sense, tell students to use the scenario to create a presentation for how to find relative frequency. Have them write out a script for their presentation, using the animation in the lesson as a guide, if necessary. Then have them present their lessons to the group.

NAME _____ DATE _____ PERIOD _____

Lesson 2 Vocabulary
Relative Frequency of Simple Events

Use the definition map to list qualities about the vocabulary word or phrase.
Sample answers are given.

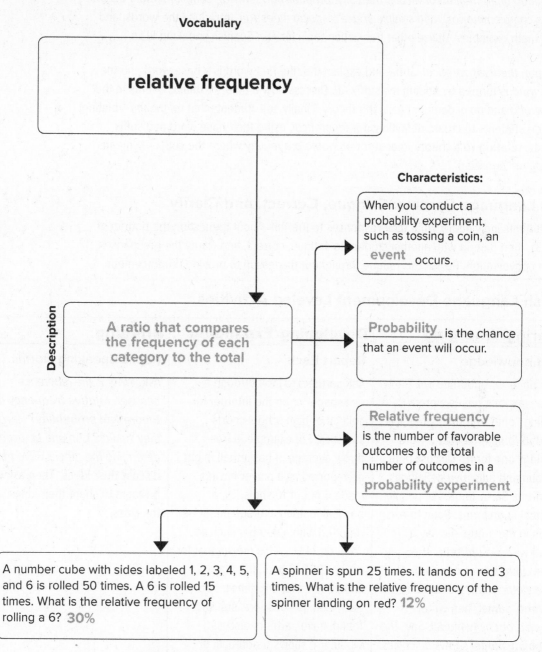

Vocabulary

relative frequency

Characteristics:

When you conduct a probability experiment, such as tossing a coin, an _____event_____ occurs.

_____Probability_____ is the chance that an event will occur.

Description

A ratio that compares the frequency of each category to the total

_____Relative frequency_____ is the number of favorable outcomes to the total number of outcomes in a _____probability experiment____.

A number cube with sides labeled 1, 2, 3, 4, 5, and 6 is rolled 50 times. A 6 is rolled 15 times. What is the relative frequency of rolling a 6? **30%**

A spinner is spun 25 times. It lands on red 3 times. What is the relative frequency of the spinner landing on red? **12%**

Write each relative frequency as a percent.

Course 2 · Module 10 *Probability* **53**

Lesson 3 Theoretical Probability of Simple Events

English Learner Instructional Strategies

Vocabulary Support: Build Background Knowledge

Write the following terms and their Spanish cognates: *uniform probability model (modelo de probabilidad uniforme), theoretical probability (probabilidad teórica), complementary events (eventos complemetarios),* and *sample space (espacio muestral).* Introduce the words, and provide math examples. Utilize other translation tools for non-Spanish speaking ELLs.

Then write: *theory/theoretical.* Show and explain that the first word is a base word and the second word is formed by adding the suffix *-al.* Discuss how a theory explains events in the natural world and an experiment tests the theory. Finally, tell students that *-al* means "relating to." Guide students to create definitions for *theoretical,* using their base word and suffix meanings. **relating to a theory** Repeat for *probable/probability* where the suffix *-ity* means "state of" or "degree of."

Math Language Routine: Critique, Correct, and Clarify

Have students individually write their responses to the Talk About It question the bottom of page 531, then pair up with another student to critique, correct, and clarify their responses through conversation. Revisit this routine throughout the lesson to provide reinforcement.

English Language Development Leveled Activities

Entering/Emerging	Developing/Expanding	Bridging
Word Knowledge Write: *uniform.* Underline *uni.* Show and explain that *uni-* is a prefix meaning "one" and that, when it is added to *form,* it creates a word meaning "one form." Discuss both the noun and adjective definitions of *uniform.* Show photos of people in matching uniforms. Point to each person in the group and say, *This person wears a* **uniform.** Then say, *All the clothes have* **one form.** *Do all the clothes look the* **same** *or* **different**? **same** Then write: *uniform probability model.* Say, *The* **probability model** *shows outcomes. The outcomes are* **uniform.** *Does each outcome have the* **same** *probability of happening?* **yes**	**Report Back** Ask partners to look through a newspaper or on the Internet for college or high school sports statistics. For example, a free-throw average in basketball might be reported as a player having made 6 out of 10 shots. Or, a baseball batting average might be reported with a number such as .245, or 24.5%—this means that for every 1,000 at bats, the player should get a hit 245 times. For each example of sports statistics found, have partners discuss whether it shows theoretical or not. Then have them report their ideas to the class.	**Public Speaking Norms** Ask, *What is the difference between* **relative frequency** *and* **theoretical probability**? *How are they similar? Can one be used to determine the other?* Have partners discuss their ideas. Then ask partners to share their ideas with the class.

NAME _____ DATE _____ PERIOD _____

Lesson 3 Vocabulary
Theoretical Probability of Simple Events

Use the three-column chart to organize the vocabulary in this lesson. Write the word in Spanish. Then write the correct terms to complete each definition.

English	Spanish	Definition
complementary events	eventos complementarios	The events of one outcome happening and that outcome not happening. The _____ sum _____ of the probabilities of an _____ event _____ and its complement is 1 or 100%.
sample space	espacio muestral	The set of all possible outcomes of a _____ probability experiment _____
theoretical probability	probabilidad teórica	The ratio of the number of ways an _____ event _____ can occur to the number of possible outcomes. It is based on what _____ should _____ happen when conducting a probability experiment.
uniform probability model	modelo de probabilidad uniforme	A probability model which assigns _____ equal _____ probability to all outcomes

Lesson 4 Compare Probabilities of Simple Events

English Learner Instructional Strategies

Graphic Support: Tables and Graphs

Tables and graphs are excellent for helping students visualize probability. Using either a spinner or a number cube, have partners conduct a probability experiment by performing 20 trials. Have them make a tally chart (table) and calculate the number of outcomes for each possible event. Then have them use the tally chart to create a graph of the results. Tell students the result for each event is the **relative probability.** Ask a student how they can use this information predict the result if they would perform 200 trials.

Math Language Routine: Discussion Supports

As students engage in discussing the Talk About It question on Student Book page 539, restate statements they make as a question to seek clarification and to confirm comprehension that the results of experiments can vary. Encourage students to challenge each other's ideas when warranted.

English Language Development Leveled Activities

For the activities below, draw a bar graph similar to the one shown:

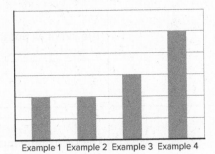

Example 1 Example 2 Example 3 Example 4

Entering/Emerging	Developing/Expanding	Bridging
Look and Identify Review the terms *greater/less than, higher/lower than, equally likely,* and *same.* Refer to the bar graph above. Say, *Compare these examples. Which has the greatest probability? Which two examples are the same?* After doing a few examples, point to two columns and say, *Compare these examples.* Students should use available language and gesturing (such as pointing) to communicate their comparison.	**Sentence Frames** Repeat the Entering/Emerging activity. Offer sentence frames for student to use for comparing the columns: ____ **and** ____ **are equally likely. The probability of** ____ **is [greater/higher/less/lower] than the probability of** ____**.**	**Building Oral Language** Have each student select one of the problems from the lesson and use available language to describe how to find the relative frequency for each outcome. Then have them compare the relative frequencies among the different possible outcomes. Make sure they use the terms *greater than, higher than, less than, lower than, equal.*

NAME _____ DATE _____ PERIOD _____

Lesson 4 Notetaking
Compare Probabilities of Simple Events

Use Cornell notes to better understand the lesson's concepts. Complete each sentence by filling in the blanks with the correct word or phrase.

Questions	Notes
1. What is the difference between theoretical probability and relative frequency?	_____Theoretical probability_____ is based on what **should** happen when conducting a probability experiment. _____Relative frequency_____ is what **actually** happens when any probability experiment is conducted.
2. What happens to the relative frequency in a probability experiment when the number of trials increases?	In a probability experiment, as the number of trial increases, the relative frequency becomes closer to the _____theoretical probability_____.

Summary

How did what you already know about relative frequency and theoretical probability help you with this lesson? See students' work.

_____

_____

_____

_____

_____

_____

_____

_____

_____

Lesson 5 Probability of Compound Events

English Learner Instructional Strategy

Graphic Support: Graphic Organizers

Before the lesson, write *compound event* and its Spanish cognate, *evento compuesto*. Introduce the words, and provide math examples. Utilize other translation tools for non-Spanish speaking ELLs. Post the words on a Word Wall.

Then write: *tree diagram*. Have students tell about different diagrams they have used in the past. Show examples, such as a Venn diagram or a plant diagram from a science textbook. Discuss how diagrams summarize and organize information. Then show a photo of a tree, along with examples of tree diagrams. Have students tell how the tree diagrams are similar to a tree. **Both have branches.** Then show how the "branches" in a tree diagram "stem" from one term, which names a characteristic the branches share.

Math Language Routine: Compare and Connect

Pair students and have them work on Examples 3 and 4 on pages 552 and 553 of the Student Book. Have them compare and contrast the processes for finding the probability of a simple event verses a compound event. Restate statements they make as a question to seek clarification and provide vocabulary or grammar prompts for students who need more guidance.

English Language Development Leveled Activities

Use the following problem with the leveled activities: *Ming rolls a number cube, tosses a coin, and chooses a card from two cards marked A and B. If an even number and heads appears, Ming wins, no matter which card is chosen. Otherwise, Lashonda wins. Find P (Ming wins).* **25%**

Entering/Emerging	Developing/Expanding	Bridging
Collaborative Support	**Turn and Talk**	**Partners Work/Pairs Check**
Have students work with a multilingual mentor on problems assigned during the lesson. Ask the mentor to help break each problem into parts. For example, for the problem above, have the mentor help the Entering/Emerging student identify these conditions for each turn in Ming's game: *1) A number cube is rolled. There are 6 possible results (rolling 1, 2, 3, 4, 5, or 6). 2) A coin is tossed. There are 2 possible results (heads or tails). 3) A card is drawn. There are 2 possible results (A or B).* Then have the student and mentor work together to set up the sample space.	Have students turn and talk with a neighbor about how to solve the problem. Encourage students to make notes about the ideas they share. Then have them respond to the question individually, using this sentence frame: **The probability that Ming will win is _____ because _____.**	Have pairs review the problem. Then ask partners to work together to write their own word problem. Tell them the word problem must be based on a game and its solution must involve setting up a sample space to find the probability of Player 1 or Player 2 winning. After students have written their problems, have them exchange papers with another pair. Tell partners to work together to solve the problem they receive. Then have them check answers with the pair who wrote the original problem.

NAME _____ DATE _____ PERIOD _____

Lesson 5 Vocabulary
Probability of Compound Events

Use the flow chart to review the process for creating a tree diagram for a compound event. Sample answers are given.

Define the phrase **compound event**.
___an event consisting of___
___two or more simple events___

Compound Event
A sandwich can be made with whole wheat or whole grain bread and three kinds of filling: peanut butter, cheese, or tuna salad.

Define the phrase **sample space**.
the set of all possible outcomes
of a probability experiment

List the Sample Space for the Compound Event
Use W for whole wheat, G for whole grain, P for peanut butter, C for cheese, and T for tuna salad.
___WP, WC, WT, GP, GC, GT___

Define the phrase **tree diagram**.
a diagram used to show the
sample space

Complete the tree diagram.

Bread	Filling	Sample Space
W	P	WP
	C	WC
	T	WT
G	P	GP
	C	GC
	T	GT

Lesson 6 Simulate Chance Events

English Learner Instructional Strategy

Sensory Support: Videos, Films, and Broadcasts

Before the lesson, write *simulation* and its Spanish cognate, *simulación*. Introduce the words, and provide math examples. Utilize other translation tools for non-Spanish speaking ELLs. Write: *simulate, simulation*. Explain that: 1) *Simulate,* a verb, is the base word of *simulation,* a noun. Use each word in a context sentence. 2) *Simulate* and *simulation* share the root word *sim,* which means "like." Discuss how the meaning "like" relates to the meanings of these words, as well as others with *sim,* such as *similar* and *simile*. Finally, show students videos of simulations and discuss how they are like dress rehearsals or re-enactments—they imitate real-life to help us prepare for the future (NASA's flight simulations for astronauts) or understand how something happened in the past (computer simulations).

Math Language Routine: Three Reads

Ensure comprehension of the Check problem on page 564 of the Student Book.
1st Read: Ensure comprehension of the meaning of *gift card*. Then make sure students understand what the store wants to do. Draw a diagram to explain the store's intention of giving a gift card to 5 out of every 8 customers that enter the store.
2nd Read: Focus students' attention on the meaning of *estimate the probability*.
3rd Read: Brainstorm ways to simulate the event.

English Language Development Leveled Activities

Entering/Emerging	Developing/Expanding	Bridging
Cooperative Learning	**Communication Guides**	**Show What You Know**
Have students work with a multilingual mentor on problems during the lesson. Ask the mentor to help students identify the conditions for each simulation and reword them, using simpler language. Then have students describe a model for simulating the outcome requested in the problem, using their native language. Have the mentors help students translate their ideas.	For each sample problem, show and discuss how each situation includes a set of conditions and a probability question. Ask partners to work together to brainstorm situations that could be represented by a simulation. Have partners choose a situation to describe and an outcome to simulate, using this communication guide: **These are the conditions: 1) ____; 2) ____; 3) ____. We want to know the probability of ____. We will use ____ to simulate the outcome. We will simulate the outcome by ____.**	Have partners choose a problem to work on together. Ask them to 1) identify the word problem's conditions and probability question, 2) discuss possible models for simulating the requested outcome, and 3) choose a model to describe. Have them make notes about how they chose their model. Then have them present their problem and solution to the class.

Multicultural Teacher Tip

Word problems are an important part of the math curriculum, but they can be particularly challenging for ELLs. When appropriate, help ELLs reword an exercise to include a familiar cultural reference.

NAME _____ DATE _____ PERIOD _____

Lesson 6 Vocabulary
Simulate Chance Events

Use the concept web to define simulation. Then give examples of different simulations from the book. Sample answers are given.

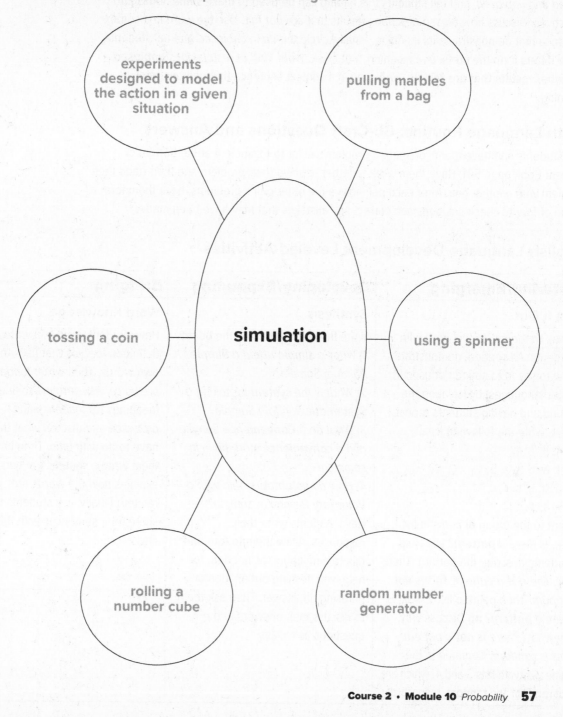

Lesson 1 Unbiased and Biased Samples
English Learner Instructional Strategy

Vocabulary Support: Activate Prior Knowledge

Before the lesson, write: *bias, biased, unbiased*. Ask, *How can a game show* **bias**? **One player has a better chance of winning than another player.** Next, underline the common letters in *biased* and *unbiased* to show that *bias* is their base word. Circle the *-ed* ending on *biased* and *unbiased,* and tell students this ending can be used to make some nouns into adjectives. Discuss how *biased* describes results that are *not fair*. Use the word in a context sentence that demonstrates its meaning. Finally, circle the *un* in *unbiased* and tell students these letters form the prefix *un-*, meaning "not." Ask, *What kind of results does* **unbiased** *describe?* **results that are fair** Use *unbiased* in a context sentence that demonstrates its meaning.

Math Language Routine: Co-Craft Questions and Answers

Pair students and have them co-create a problem similar to Example 4 at the bottom of Student Book page 581. Have them work together to solve their problem and then trade their problem with another pair. After each pair solves the other pair's problems, have them form a group of four to check solutions and correct any mistakes that may have been made.

English Language Development Leveled Activities

Entering/Emerging	Developing/Expanding	Bridging
Act It Out	**Synthesis**	**Word Knowledge**
Write: *random*. Say the word with students. As needed, demonstrate how to say /r/ (a sound not used in some languages) by isolating the sound and having students repeat. Next, write the following lists: 1) 1, 3, 2, 4; 2) 1, w, 6, x, z, 5; 3) a, a, b, b, c, c; 4) *, &, #, %, *, ^. Point to the group of items in list 1. Ask, *Is there a* **pattern? yes** Help students describe the pattern. Then say, *There* **is** *a pattern. This is* **not** *random.* Then point to list 2. Ask, *Is there a* **pattern**? **no** Discuss why. Then say, *There* **is not** *a pattern. This is* **random.** Continue in the same way with lists 3 and 4, which are **not random** and **random,** respectively.	Write these questions on the board: 1) *What is* **simple** *about a* **Simple** *Random Sample?* 2) *What is the* **system** *for taking a* **Systematic** *Random Sample?* 3) *What do a* **Convenience** *Sample and a* **convenience** *store have in common?* 4) *How do* **volunteers** *help with a* **Voluntary** *Response Sample?* Have students write their responses. Allow them to turn and talk to a neighbor, as needed, for help with fleshing out an idea or phrasing an answer. Then ask them to discuss their answers to the questions as a class.	Have students help you write a definition for *bias* that uses their own words. Then write: *tendency, prejudice*. Ask partners to find the meanings for *tendency* and *prejudice* and discuss what they have to do with *bias*. Then have them write a sentence of two that explains how the words are related. Finally, ask students to share their sentences with the class.

NAME _____ DATE _____ PERIOD _____

Lesson 1 Vocabulary

Unbiased and Biased Samples

Use the three-column chart to organize the vocabulary in this lesson. Write the
word in Spanish. Then write the definition of each word. Sample answers are given.

English	Spanish	Definition
unbiased sample	muestra no sesgada	a sample representative of the entire population
simple random sample	muestra aleatoria simple	an unbiased sample where each item or person in the population is as likely to be chosen as any other
systematic random sample	muestra aleatoria sistemática	a sample where the items or people are selected according to a specific time or item interval
biased sample	muestra sesgada	a sample drawn in such a way that one or more parts of the population are favored over others
convenience sample	muestra de conveniencia	a sample which consists of members of a population that are easily accessed
voluntary response sample	muestra de repuesta voluntaria	a sample which involves only those who want to participate in the sampling

Lesson 2 Make Predictions

English Learner Instructional Strategy

Vocabulary Support: Cognates

Before the lesson, write *population* and *statistics* and their Spanish cognates, *población* and *estadística,* respectively. Introduce the words, and provide math examples. Utilize other translation tools for non-Spanish speaking ELLs. Post the words on a Word Wall. Underline *pop* in *population.* Tell students that *pop* is a root word that means "people." Help students relate the meaning of the root word to the meaning of *population.* Share examples of other words with *pop,* such as *popular* and *populous,* and relate their meanings to the meaning of the root. Finally, have students write their own definitions for *population* and *statistics* in their notebooks. Encourage them to include with each definition a sentence, using the vocabulary word in context, and an illustration to help them remember the word's meaning.

Math Language Routine: Stronger and Clearer Each Time

Have students individually write their responses to the Talk About It question on Student Book page 585, then pair up with another student to refine and clarify their responses through conversation. Students then revise their initial written responses and repeat with a new partner.

English Language Development Leveled Activities

Entering/Emerging	Developing/Expanding	Bridging
Basic Vocabulary	**Act It Out**	**Public Speaking Norms**
Before the lesson, show and explain the meanings of these words, found in this lesson's word problems: *athletic, baseball, softball, basketball, football, gymnastics, tennis, volleyball, defects, Smart watches, non-profit, volunteer, lasagna, jeans, capris, athletic pants, banana, blueberry, honeydew.* Teaching students this basic vocabulary prior to the lesson will help them to focus their attention on instruction during the lesson.	Have partners work together to brainstorm survey questions they could use to find out more about their classmates' interests or preferences. After they have had some time to think, tell partners to choose one question to write and then pass their question around for classmates to answer. Once their surveys have circulated throughout the class, have partners chart the responses in a table they create. Finally, have them find the probability for each survey response, based on their sample.	Ask, *What is a prediction?* **Sample response: A statement telling something that is likely to happen in the future.** Then post these questions: *What are examples of predictions you have heard people make? On what facts did the people base their predictions? When and why might you make a prediction? What makes predictions reliable? How can mathematics make a prediction more reliable?* Have students discuss their responses to these questions with a neighbor. Then ask them to share their ideas and experiences with the class.

Lesson 2 Vocabulary

Make Predictions

Use the vocabulary squares to write a definition, a sentence, and an example for each vocabulary word. Sample answers are given.

statistics	Definition
	the study of collecting, organizing, and interpreting data
Example	**Sentence**
Sixty-five percent of the students surveyed said their favorite subject is math.	Using statistics, you can get information about a population and find trends in data.

survey	Definition
	a question or set of questions designed to collect data about a specific group of people, or population
Example	**Sentence**
1. What grade are you in? 2. Who is your teacher? 3. Do you prefer pizza or pasta?	The survey included questions about grade, teacher, and food.

population	Definition
	the entire group of items or individuals from which the samples under consideration are taken
Example	**Sentence**
7th graders at Beacon Middle School	The population included all 7th grade students in the school.

Lesson 3 Multiple Samples

English Learner Instructional Strategy

Graphic Support: Graphic Organizers

Draw a *Mean* definition web on an anchor chart or word wall. Help students complete the web by writing a definition for the statiscal mean, listing characteristics of the mean, and showing examples of how to find the mean. Tell students that in this lesson, they will be finding the mean of more than one set of numbers, or the mean of multiple samples of the same population.

For *variability,* have volunteers draw an example graph for one of the following: *high variability, low variability, no variability.* Ask students to use available language to describe each graph.

Entering/Emerging students can point, say yes/no, or give short responses.

Developing/Expanding students can use simple sentences: **The first graph shows _____.**

Bridging students can use more complex language: **The first graph shows _____ because _____.**

Math Language Routine: Collect and Display

As students discuss the Learn activity on Student Book pages 593-596, write key words and phrases you hear, such as *mean, samples, variability,* and *distribution.* Display the words and phrases for student reference throughout the lesson. Update the collection with other relevant terms and new understandings as the lesson progresses.

English Language Development Leveled Activities

Entering/Emerging	Developing/Expanding	Bridging
Look, Listen, and Identify	**Listen and Identify**	**Academic Vocabulary**
Draw examples of *high, low,* and *no variability.* Ask, *Which one shows high variability?* Students should point to the correct graph. When they have identified the correct graph, model and prompt students to say **high variability.** Repeat until students are firm in their understanding and can clearly pronounce each term.	Give clues about any of the following vocabulary and have students identify the term: *biased sample, unbiased sample, convenience sample, voluntary response sample, variability, high/low/no variability.* For example, say, *All responses in the sample are the same.* **no variability** Depending on students' abilities, challenge them to provide the clues to a partner.	Have students create or add to an anchor chart to cover all of the words learned in the module so far. Assign one or more words to each student and have them write the word, its cognate, a definition, and an example for each term. Then have them share their work with a partner to discuss any revisions. Finally share with the group before adding the information to the anchor chart.

NAME _____ DATE _____ PERIOD _____

Lesson 3 Vocabulary
Generate Multiple Samples

Use the definition map to list qualities about the vocabulary word or phrase.
Sample answers are given.

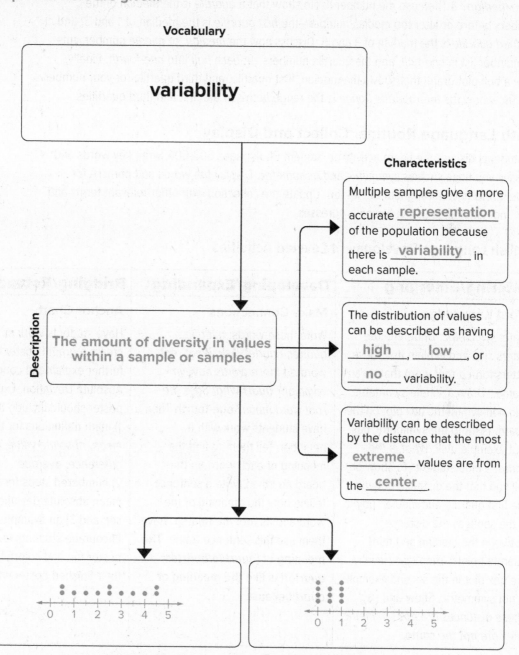

Vocabulary

variability

Characteristics

Multiple samples give a more accurate <u>representation</u> of the population because there is <u>variability</u> in each sample.

Description

The amount of diversity in values within a sample or samples

The distribution of values can be described as having <u>high</u>, <u>low</u>, or <u>no</u> variability.

Variability can be described by the distance that the most <u>extreme</u> values are from the <u>center</u>.

Examples of two dot plots with different variability.

Lesson 4 Compare Two Populations
English Learner Instructional Strategy

Graphic Support: Graphs

Before the lesson, write: *first quartile, third quartile, interquartile range.* Discuss how these terms are related. First, underline the letters *quart* in each of the terms, and tell students these letters form a root word meaning "one-fourth." Next, write: 1, 2, 3, 3, 3, 4, 5. Ask, *What is the **median**?* **3** Then use the number list to show that a *quartile* is the median of the numbers before or after the median number—the *first quartile* is the median of 1 and 3, and the *third quartile* is the median of 3 and 5. Discuss how the *median,* or *middle* number, cuts the number list in *one-half,* and the quartile numbers cut each *half* into *one-fourth.* Finally, draw a box-plot graph that shows the median, first quartile, and third quartile for your number list. Show how the *Interquartile Range* is the range *between* the first and third quartilies.

Math Language Routine: Collect and Display

As students discuss the Learn activity on Student Book pages 603-604, write key words and phrases you hear, such as *symmetric* and *asymmetric.* Display the words and phrases for student reference throughout the lesson. Update the collection with other relevant terms and new understandings as the lesson progresses.

English Language Development Leveled Activities

Entering/Emerging	Developing/Expanding	Bridging/Reteaching
Word Knowledge	**Make Connections**	**Anchor Chart**
Write: *symmetric.* Underline the letters *sym* and explain that these letters form a root word that means "same." Draw a simple symmetric and non-symmetric box plot on the board. Point to the symmetric box plot example. Ask, *What is the **same**?* Guide students to show or tell you that the distance between the first quartile and median points is the same as the distance between the median and third quartile points. Then discuss why the box plot in the second example is not symmetric. Show and say, *These distances are **not** symmetric. They are **not** the **same.***	Write these words: *quartile, quarter, quartet.* Ask, *What root word do these words have in common?* **quart** *What does the root word mean?* **one-fourth** Then have students work with a neighbor. Tell them to find the meaning of each word on the board and then write a sentence telling how the meaning of the word and its root are related. Have them use this sentence frame: **The meaning of [*quartile/quarter/quartet*] is like the meaning of *quart* because _____.**	Have students work as a group to create a graffiti poster that helps further explain the concept of Mean Absolute Deviation. Explain that the poster should include the following: 1) math definitions for these terms: *mean, absolute value, deviation, difference, average;* 2) numbered steps for finding the mean absolute deviation of a data set; and 3) an example problem. Encourage students to make their poster fun and colorful. Discuss their finished poster with the class.

NAME _____ DATE _____ PERIOD _____

Lesson 4 Vocabulary
Compare Two Populations

Use the word cards to define each vocabulary word or phrase and give an
example. Sample answers are given.

Word Cards

double box plot	doble diagrama de caja
Definition	**Definición**
two box plots graphed on the same number line	dos diagramas de caja sobre la misma recta numérica
Example Sentence	
You can draw inferences about two populations using a double box plot to compare their centers and variations.	

Word Cards

double dot plot	doble diagrama de puntos
Definition	**Definición**
a distribution of two sets of data values where each value is shown as a dot above a number line	una distribución de dos conjuntos de valores donde cada valor se muestra como un punto arriba de una recta numérica
Example Sentence	
A double dot plot uses the same number line to draw inferences about two populations.	

Lesson 5 Assess Visual Overlap
English Learner Instructional Strategy

Vocabulary Support: Build Background Knowledge

Write *visual overlap* on the board or Word Wall. Ask, *What does* visual *mean?* Give students a chance to answer. Then, if necessary, say, *Visual describes something related to sight or that can be seen.* Then demonstrate the meaning of *overlap* using two sheets of paper. Slide one sheet partly over the other and point to where they overlap. Say, *This part of the paper* **overlaps** *the other part.* **Overlap** *is the area where one thing partly covers another thing.* Say, *Visual overlap means you can see where the overlap is.* Say *visual overlap* and have students chorally repeat.

Write *assess* on the board and provide more familiar synonyms or related phrases to help clarify the meaning, such *evaluate, estimate, get an idea of, judge, consider.* Provide a nonmath example of *assess,* such as assessing a situation: *I can* **assess** *the weather by looking outside to see what the sky looks like, what other people are wearing, how strong the wind is blowing.* Explain that to *assess visual overlap* means comparing two sets of data to get an idea of how similar or different the means are likely to be.

Math Language Routine: Discussion Supports

As students engage in discussing the Talk About It question on Student Book page 613, restate statements they make as a question to seek clarification and to confirm comprehension, providing validation or correction when necessary. Encourage students to challenge each other's ideas when warranted, as well as to elaborate on their ideas and give examples.

English Language Development Leveled Activities

Entering/Emerging	Developing/Expanding	Bridging
Word Knowledge	**Echo Reading**	**Round the Table**
Review *mean* and *mean absolute deviation (MAD).* Provide a dot plot with the following values: 2, 2, 3, 3, 4, 4, 4, 4, 5, 5, 6, 6. Ask, *How do we find the mean?* Prompt students to say **mean**. Model finding the mean (4), and then ask, *What is the mean?* Have students use a sentence frame: **The _____ is _____.** Repeat the process to review *mean absolute deviation.*	During the Check portion of the lesson, have students take turns echo reading the text. Start by reading through the entire problem one time. Then read it again, one sentence at a time, having students take turns echo reading each sentence after you. Be sure to read slowly and enunciate clearly. Provide feedback about correct pronunciation. As you guide students through solving the problem, have them continue echoing your explanations of each step.	On the board, display two dot plots with the following data: Plot 1: 15, 15, 16, 16, 16, 17, 17, 17, 18, 18; Plot 2: 17, 18, 18, 19, 19, 19, 19, 20, 20, 21. Then organize students in groups of four. Assign one student to be the "teacher." Have the three "students" assess the degree of visual overlap between the data sets. Each student will complete one step in the solving process before passing the paper on to the next student. When the problem has been solved, the "teacher" should review the work to ensure that it was correct and fix any errors. Then ask the "teachers" to present their work to the class.

NAME _____ DATE _____ PERIOD _____

Lesson 5 Vocabulary
Assess Visual Overlap

Use the definition map to write a description and list characteristics about the vocabulary word or phrase. Write or draw math examples. Share your examples with a classmate.

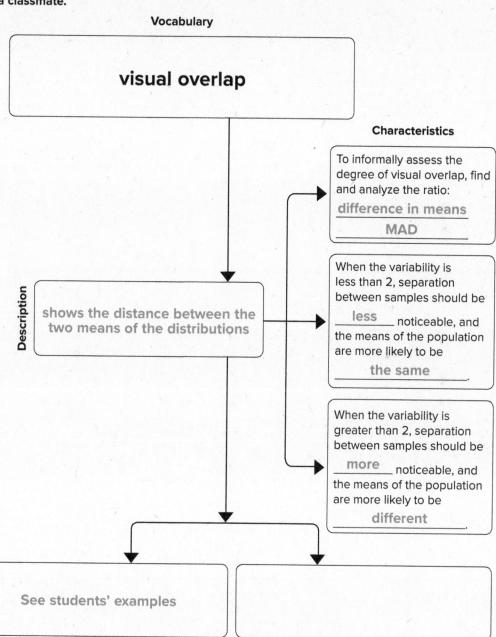

Vocabulary

visual overlap

Characteristics

To informally assess the degree of visual overlap, find and analyze the ratio:

$$\frac{\text{difference in means}}{\text{MAD}}$$

When the variability is less than 2, separation between samples should be _____less_____ noticeable, and the means of the population are more likely to be _____the same_____.

When the variability is greater than 2, separation between samples should be _____more_____ noticeable, and the means of the population are more likely to be _____different_____.

Description

shows the distance between the two means of the distributions

See students' examples

Example of dot plots with visual overlap.

Dinah Zike Explaining
Visual Kinesthetic Vocabulary®, or VKVs®

What are VKVs and who needs them?

"VKVs are flashcards that animate words by kinesthetically focusing on their structure, use, and meaning. VKVs are beneficial not only to students learning the specialized vocabulary of a content area, but also to students learning the vocabulary of a second language."

Dinah Zike | Educational Consultant

Dinah-Might Activities, Inc. – San Antonio, Texas

Why did you invent VKVs?

"Twenty years ago, I began designing flashcards that would accomplish the same thing with academic vocabulary and cognates that Foldables® do with general information, concepts, and ideas—make them a visual, kinesthetic, and memorable experience."

Dinah Zike's
Visual
Kinesthetic
Vocabulary

I had three goals in mind:

- **Making two-dimensional flashcards three-dimensional**

- **Designing flashcards that allow one or more parts of a word or phrase to be manipulated and changed to form numerous terms based upon a commonality**

- **Using one sheet or strip of paper to make purposefully shaped flashcards that were neither glued nor stapled, but could be folded to the same height, making them easy to stack and store**

Why are VKVs important in today's classroom?

"At the beginning of this century, research and reports indicated the importance of vocabulary to overall academic achievement. This research resulted in a more comprehensive teaching of academic vocabulary and a focus on the use of cognates to help students learn a second language. Teachers know the importance of using a variety of strategies to teach vocabulary to a diverse population of students. VKVs function as one of those strategies."

An Interview with

**Dinah Zike Explaining
Visual Kinesthetic Vocabulary®, or VKVs®**

Dinah Zike's
Visual
Kinesthetic
Vocabulary

How are VKVs used to teach content vocabulary to EL students?

" VKVs can be used to show the similarities between cognates in Spanish and English. For example, by folding and unfolding specially designed VKVs, students can experience English terms in one color and Spanish in a second color on the same flashcard while noting the similarities in their roots. "

What organization and usage hints would you give teachers using VKVs?

" Cut off the flap of a 6" x 9" envelope and slightly widen the envelope's opening by cutting away a shallow V or half circle on one side only. Glue the non-cut side of the envelope into the front or back of student notebooks or journals. VKVs can be stored in this pocket.

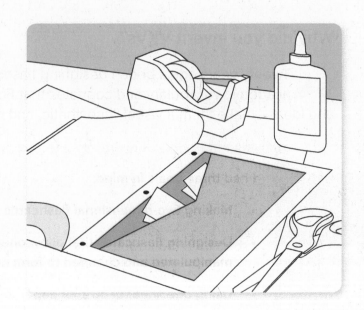

Encourage students to individualize their flashcards by writing notes, sketching diagrams, recording examples, forming plurals (radius: radii or radiuses), and noting when the math terms presented are homophones (sine/sign) or contain root words or combining forms (kilo-, milli-, tri-).

As students make and use the flashcards included in this text, they will learn how to design their own VKVs. Provide time for students to design, create, and share their flashcards with classmates. "

Dinah Zike's book Foldables, Notebook Foldables, & VKVs for Spelling and Vocabulary 4th-12th won a Teachers' Choice Award in 2011 for "instructional value, ease of use, quality, and innovation"; it has become a popular methods resource for teaching and learning vocabulary.

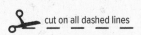
Solve the proportion. (Resuelve una proporción.)

$$\frac{6}{x} = \frac{5}{8}$$

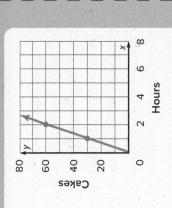

Does the graph show a direct variation? Explain. (¿El gráfico muestra una variación directa? Explique.)

proportion

proporción

direct

variación

In math, a proportion is an equation stating that (en matemáticas, una proporción es una ecuación que indica que).

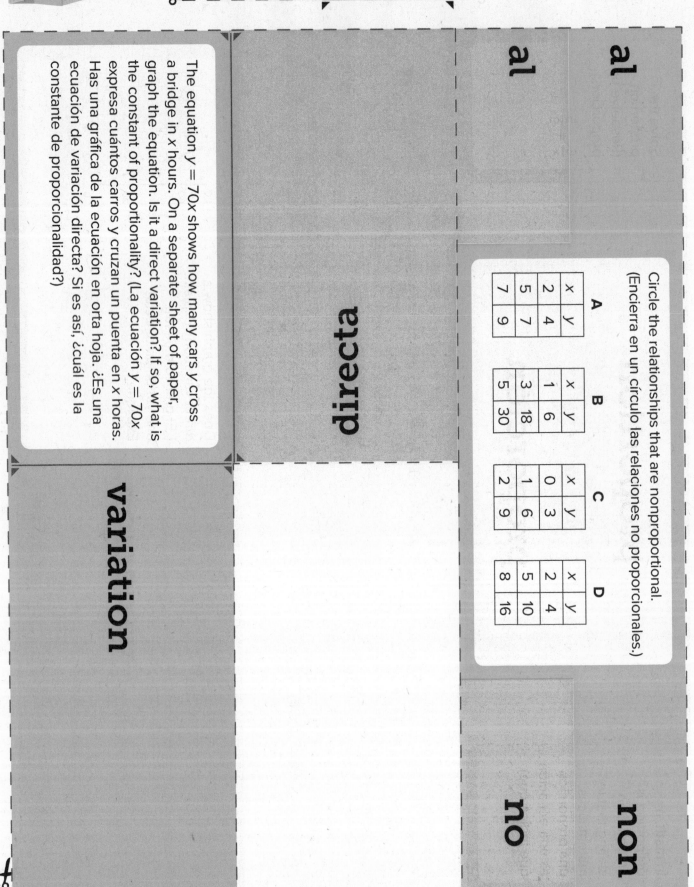

al

al

al

directa

variation

no

non

The equation $y = 70x$ shows how many cars y cross a bridge in x hours. On a separate sheet of paper, graph the equation. Is it a direct variation? If so, what is the constant of proportionality? (La ecuación $y = 70x$ expresa cuántos carros y cruzan un puente en x horas. Has una gráfica de la ecuación en orta hoja. ¿Es una ecuación de variación directa? Si es así, ¿cuál es la constante de proporcionalidad?)

Circle the relationships that are nonproportional. (Encierra en un círculo las relaciones no proporcionales.)

A

x	y
2	4
5	7
7	9

B

x	y
1	6
3	18
5	30

C

x	y
0	3
1	6
2	9

D

x	y
2	4
5	10
8	16

Define percent error.
(Define porcentaje de error.)

_____

_____

_____

percent error

Write each number as a percent. (Escribar cada número como un porcentaje.)

$0.25 =$ _____ %

$\dfrac{5}{6} =$ _____ %

$12 =$ _____ %

$\dfrac{9}{10} =$ _____ %

de error

Sofia estimated that a drive to the beach would take 3 hours. The actual drive lasted for 3 hours and 25 minutes. What was the percent error of Sofia's estimate? (Sofía calculó que un recorrido en auto hasta la playa tardaría 3 horas. El recorrido real tardó 3 horas y 25 minutos. ¿Cual fue el porcentaje de error en el cálculo de Sofía?)

Answer: about _____ %

porcentaje

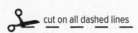

Write the additive inverse of each number below. (Escribe el inverso aditivo de los siguientes números.)

13 _____ −2 _____

−25 _____ 1 _____

additive inverse

Define additive inverse. (Define inverso aditivo.)

Define absolute value. (Define valor absoluto.)

absolute value

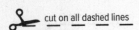

aditivo

inverso

valor absoluto

Circle the word that has the same meaning as *additive inverse*. (Encierra en un círculo la palabra que significa lo mismo que inverso aditivo.)

negative integer   opposite

number line   absolute value

Evaluate each expression. (Evalúa cada expresión.)

|−23| = _____

|8| = _____

|−16| − |9| = _____

|−7| + |10| = _____

Write the opposite of each number below.
(Escribe el opuesto de los siguientes números.)

12 _____   −54 _____

−16 _____   25 _____

Explain how to graph an integer on a number line. (Explica cómo representar gráficamente un entero en una recta numérica.)

opposites

graph

Dinah Zike's
Visual Kinesthetic Vocabulary

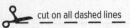

✂ cut on all dashed lines   ⬚ fold on all solid lines

ficar

uestos

Graph −6, 2, 8, and −3 on the number line. (Representa gráficamente −6, 2, 8, y −3 en la recta numérica.)

−8 −6 −4 −2 0 2 4 6 8 10 12

Explain why 6 and −6 are opposites. (Explica por qué 6 y −6 son opuestos.)

VKV10   Visual Kinesthetic Learning

Why is bar notation used to represent repeating decimals? (¿Por qué la notación de barras se utiliza para representar números decimales periódicos?)

bar notation

What does the bar in 0.1$\overline{6}$ mean? (¿Qué significa la barra sobre 0.1$\overline{6}$?)

How does writing fractions with a common denominator help you compare them? (¿De qué forma escribir fracciones con un común denominador te ayuda a compararlas entre sí?)

common denominator

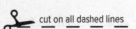

de barra

común denominador

Use bar notation to rewrite each decimal. (Vuelve a escribir cada número decimal con notación de barras.)

$0.7777\ldots =$ _____

$9.3555\ldots =$ _____

$-0.337337\ldots =$ _____

Rewrite $\frac{1}{8}$ and $\frac{1}{5}$ with a common denominator.

(Escribe $\frac{1}{8}$ y $\frac{1}{5}$ de manera que ambos tengan un común denominador.)

$$\frac{1}{8} = $$ _____

$$\frac{1}{5} = $$ _____

notación

rational number

Define rational number. (Define número racional.)

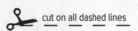 cut on all dashed lines

□ fold on all solid lines

número racional

List three different forms of rational numbers. (Enumera tres formas de representar los números racionales.)

Dinah Zike's
Visual
Kinesthetic
Vocabulary
VKV

✂ cut on all dashed lines   fold on all solid lines

coefficient

Define coefficient. (Define coeficiente.)

Rewrite $9x - 15y$ in factored form. (Escribe la forma factorizada de la función $9x - 15y$.)

factored form

What property is used when factoring a linear expression? (¿Qué propiedad se utiliza para factorizar una función lineal?)

Circle the greatest common factor of $15x$ and $27xy$. (Encierra en un círculo el máximo común divisor de $15x$ y $27xy$.)

3	3x	y
5	x	9

factor

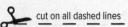
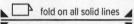
iciente

factorizada

izar

Circle the coefficient in each expression. (Encierra en un círculo el coeficiente de cada expresión.)

$12 - 5x$

$19m - 24$

$9p + 17r$

$37 + 11a$

Write about a time when writing a linear expression in factored form might be useful. (Escribe sobre una situación en la que sería útil escribir la forma factorizada de una función lineal.)

forma

Factor each expression. (Factoriza cada expresión.)

$12x + 3 =$ _____

$27a + 12b =$ _____

$16m - 18 =$ _____

Dinah Zike's
Visual
Kinesthetic
Vocabulary
VKV

cut on all dashed lines

fold on all solid lines

Find the GCF of the pair of monomials. (Halla el MCD de ambos monomios.)

6x, 21xy

_____

expression

monomial

lineal

Is $a^2 - 6$ a linear expression? Explain. (¿Es la expresión $a^2 - 6$ una función lineal? Explica.)

Dinah Zike's
Visual
Kinesthetic
Vocabulary

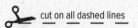 cut on all dashed lines

fold on all solid lines

expresión

linear

Write two examples of linear expressions. (Escribe dos ejemplos de funciones lineales.)

Define monomial. (Define monomio.)

Dinah Zike's
VKV Visual
Kinesthetic
Vocabulary

✂ cut on all dashed lines

fold on all solid lines

What value of x makes the equation true? (¿Qué valor de x hace la ecuación verdadera?)

$x + 8 = 13$

_____

solution

Circle the equations that are equivalent to $x = 9$. (Encierra en un círculo las ecuaciones equivalentes a $x = 9$.)

$x + 12 = 20$ $x - 5 = 4$ $3 + x = 12$

equivalent equation

Dinah Zike's
Visual
Kinesthetic
Vocabulary

✂ cut on all dashed lines

⬜ fold on all solid lines

ción

ecuación equivalente

Find the solution of each equation. (Halla la solución de cada ecuación.)

$x - 12 = 8$ _____

$9 + y = 17$ _____

Are the equations $x + 11 = 14$ and $x = 3$ equivalent? Explain. (¿Son las ecuaciones $x + 11 = 14$ and $x = 3$ equivalentes? Explica.)

_____
_____
_____

How many planes intersect to form a cube?
(¿Cuantos planos se intersecan en un cubo?)

_____

cube

Define congruent. (Define congruente.)

_____
_____
_____

Cones and cylinders are not polyhedrons. Explain why. (Explica por qué los conos y los cilindros no son poliedros.)

_____
_____

plane

cone

congruent

Dinah Zike's
Visual
Kinesthetic
Vocabulary

✂ cut on all dashed lines

▢ fold on all solid lines

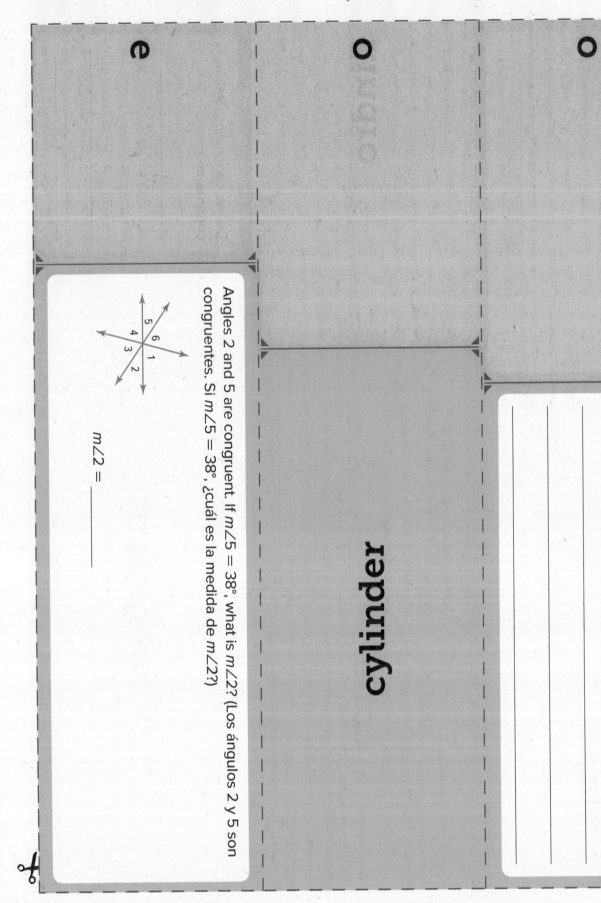

e

o

ángulo

o

Angles 2 and 5 are congruent. If $m\angle 5 = 38°$, what is $m\angle 2$? (Los ángulos 2 y 5 son congruentes. Si $m\angle 5 = 38°$, ¿cuál es la medida de $m\angle 2$?)

$m\angle 2 =$ _____

cylinder

Other than being flat, a plane has no shape. Explain why. (Explica por qué un plano no tiene forma a pesar de ser plano.)

scale model

factor de

What is the scale factor of a dollhouse if 5 centimeters represents 1 meter? (¿Cuál es el factor de escala de una casa de muñecas en la que 5 centímetros representan un metro?)

Dinah Zike's
Visual Kinesthetic Vocabulary

✂ ---- cut on all dashed lines

▶ 🗁 fold on all solid lines ◀

modelo a escala

factor

List three examples where you might find scale models used. (Menciona tres situaciones en las que se utilizan modelos a escala.)

Copyright © McGraw-Hill Education.

Dinah Zike's
VKV Visual
Kinesthetic
Vocabulary

cut on all dashed lines

fold on all solid lines

center

nferencia

circle

Define center. (Define centro.)

Define circle. (Define círculo.)

circumference

írculo

Find the circumference. (Halla la circunferencia.)

15 m

Use center to describe the radius and diameter of a circle. (Utiliza la palabra *centro* para describir el radio y el diámetro de un círculo.)

ro

A circle's diameter is _____ the length of the circle's radius. (El diámetro de un círculo es el _____ de la longitud del radio del círculo.)

If you know the length of a circle's radius, what three other measurements can you find? (¿Cuáles tres medidas puedes calcular con la longitud del radio de un círculo?)

_____
_____
_____

Describe a real-world composite figure, explaining the object's purpose, and the figures of which it is composed. (Describe un objeto real cuya forma sea una figura compuesta. Explica su función y menciona las figuras de las cuales se compone.)

diameter

radius

composite figure

Define composite figure. (Define figura compuesto.)

_____
_____
_____

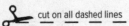

✂ cut on all dashed lines

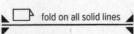

fold on all solid lines

compuesto

o

ámetro

Use two polygons to draw a composite figure. (Dibuja una figura compuesta por dos polígonos.)

Draw a radius of the circle. (Dibuja el radio del círculo.)

Draw a diameter of the circle. (Dibuja el diámetro del círculo.)

figura

 Dinah Zike's
Visual
Kinesthetic
Vocabulary

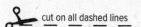 cut on all dashed lines   fold on all solid lines

The formula for the area of a circle is $A = \pi r^2$. Write the formula for the area of a semicircle. (La fórmula para calcular el área de un círculo es $A = \pi r^2$. Escribe la fórmula para calcular el área de un semicírculo.)

$A = $ _____

semicircle

Define lateral surface area. (Define área de superficie lateral.)

lateral surface area

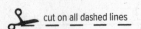 cut on all dashed lines

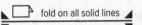 fold on all solid lines

írculo

área de superficie lateral

Find the area of the semicircle. (Calcula el área del semicírculo.)

14 yd

Find the lateral surface area of the figure. Use the formula $L.A. = \frac{1}{2}P\ell$ (Utiliza la fórmula $S.L. = \frac{1}{2}P\ell$ para calcular la superficie lateral de la figura.)

16 m
16 m
20 m
16 m

 cut on all dashed lines

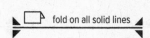 fold on all solid lines

regular pyramid

The base of a regular pyramid is a regular
(La base de una pirámide regular es un
regular.)
_____.

cut on all dashed lines

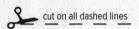
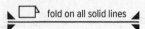
pirámide regular

Define regular pyramid. (Define pirámide regular.)

✂ cut on all dashed lines

fold on all solid lines

Define simulation. (Define simulación.)

simulation

Dinah Zike's
Visual
Kinesthetic
Vocabulary

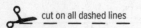
cut on all dashed lines

fold on all solid lines

ción

Describe a model to represent choosing one pair of socks at random from a drawer with six pairs total. (Describe un modelo que represente la elección al azar de un par de calcetines en un cajón de seis pares de calcetines.)

Dinah Zike's
Visual
Kinesthetic
Vocabulary

cut on all dashed lines

fold on all solid lines

theoretical probability

experimental

What is the theoretical probability of rolling a 3 with a number cube? (¿Cuál es la probabilidad teórica de obtener un 3 al lanzar un dado?)

_____

probabilidad teórica

experimental

Using a number cube, you roll a 5 four times out of 18 total rolls. What is the experimental probability of rolling another 5? (En dieciocho lanzamientos de un dado, obtienes un 5 cuatro veces. ¿Cuál es la probabilidad experimental de obtener otro 5?)

Dinah Zike's
Visual
Kinesthetic
Vocabulary

✂ cut on all dashed lines

▢ fold on all solid lines

Define population. (Define población.)

statistics

population

Dinah Zike's
Visual
Kinesthetic
Vocabulary

VKV

✂ cut on all dashed lines   fold on all solid lines

ción

dística

Statistics deal with _____, and _____ data. (La estadística tiene que ver con _____ y _____ de datos.)

e

You want to survey customers at a store to see which dog food is most popular.

The population is _____. The sample is _____.

(Vas a hacer una encuesta a los clientes de un almacén para averiguar cuál comida para perros es más popular.

La población es _____. La muestra es _____.)

VKV Answer Appendix

VKV3
proportion: $x = 9.6$; two ratios or rates are equivalent
variación: yes; See students' work.

VKV4
nonproportional: A, C
variation: See students' graphs; yes; 70

VKV5
percent error: 25; $83\frac{1}{3}$; 1200; 90; See students' work.

VKV6
porcentaje de error: 13.9

VKV7
absolute value: See students' work for definition.
additive inverse: See students' work for definition; -13; 2; 25; -1

VKV8
valor absoluto: 23; 8; 17; 7
inverso aditivo: opposite

VKV9
graph: Sample answer: draw a dot on the line at its location.
opposites: -12; 54; 16; -25

VKV10
graficar: See students' work for graphs.
opuestos: Sample answer: 6 and -6 are 6 are the same distance away from 0, but on opposite sides of 0 on the number line, therefore they are opposites.

VKV11
bar notation: Sample answers: It means that the 6 repeats forever; It would be impossible to continue writing a repeating decimal forever, so we have a symbol to show us that the number(s) repeat(s) forever.
common denominator: See students' work.

VKV12
notación de barra: $0.\overline{7}$; $9.3\overline{5}$; $-0.\overline{337}$
común denominador: $\frac{5}{40}$ and $\frac{8}{40}$

VKV13
rational number: See students' work for definition.

VKV14
número racional: Sample answer: fractional, repeating decimal, whole number.

VKV15
coefficient: See students' work for definition.
factor: $3x$
factored form: The Distributive Property; See students' work.

VKV16
coeficiente: -5; 19; 9 and 17; 11
factorizar: $3(4x + 1)$; $3(9a + 4b)$; $2(8m - 9)$
forma factorizada: See students' work.

VKV17
linear expression: no; Sample answer: when a variable is squared, the graph of the expression does not form a straight line.
monomial: $3x$

VKV18
expresión lineal: Sample answer: $x + 3$, $4y - 7$
monomio: See students' work for definition.

VKV19
equivalent equation: $x - 5 = 4$; $3 + x = 12$
solution: 5

VKV20
equación equivalente: Sample answer: yes; the equation $x + 11 = 14$ can be simplified to $x = 3$.
solución: 20; 8

VKV21

cone: Sample answer: cones and cylinders have faces that are circles and polyhedron must have only faces that are polygons.
congruent: See students' work for definition.
plane: 6

VKV22

congruente: 38°
plano: Sample answer: a plane extends in all directions forever, therefore it does not have edges to make a shape.

VKV23

scale model: $\frac{1}{20}$

VKV24

modelo a escala: See students' work for examples.

VKV25

center: See students' work for definition.
circle: See students' work for definition.

VKV26

centro: See students' work.
circumference: about 47.1 m

VKV27

composite figure: See students' work for definition; See students' work.
diameter: twice
radius: diameter, circumference, area

VKV28

figura compuesto: See students' drawings.
diámetro: See students' work.
radio: See students' work.

VKV29

lateral surface area: See students' work for definition.
semicircle: $A = \frac{1}{2}\pi r^2$ or $\frac{\pi r^2}{2}$

VKV30

area de superficie lateral: 480 m²
semicírculo: about 307.72 yd²

VKV31

regular pyramid: polygon

VKV32

pirámide regular: See students' work for definition.

VKV33

simulation: See students' work for definition.

VKV34

simulación: See students' work.

VKV35

theoretical probability: $\frac{1}{6}$

VKV36

probabilidad teórica: $\frac{4}{18}$ or $\frac{2}{9}$

VKV37

population: See students' work for definition.

VKV38

populación: customers at a store; Sample answer: every third customer who walks through the front door
estadística: collecting; organizing; interpreting